MARRIAGE BONDS
and
MINISTERS' RETURNS
of
PRINCE EDWARD COUNTY, VIRGINIA
1754-1810

Catherine Lindsay Knorr

JANAWAY PUBLISHING, INC.
Santa Maria, California

> **Notice**
>
> In many older books, foxing (or discoloration) occurs and, in some instances, print lightens with wear and age. Reprinted books, such as this, often duplicate these flaws, notwithstanding efforts to reduce or eliminate them. The pages of this reprint have been digitally enhanced and, where possible, the flaws eliminated in order to provide clarity of content and a pleasant reading experience.

Copyright © Catherine Lindsay Knorr, 1950

Originally published:
Pine Bluff, Arkansas
1950

Reprinted by:

Janaway Publishing, Inc.
732 Kelsey Ct.
Santa Maria, California 93454
(805) 925-1038
www.JanawayGenealogy.com

2006, 2012

ISBN: 978-1-59641-123-4

Made in the United States of America

To

Annie Bocage Proctor

(Mrs. Feaster Le Grande Proctor)

my matchless sister:

That kinship being my sole claim to fame.

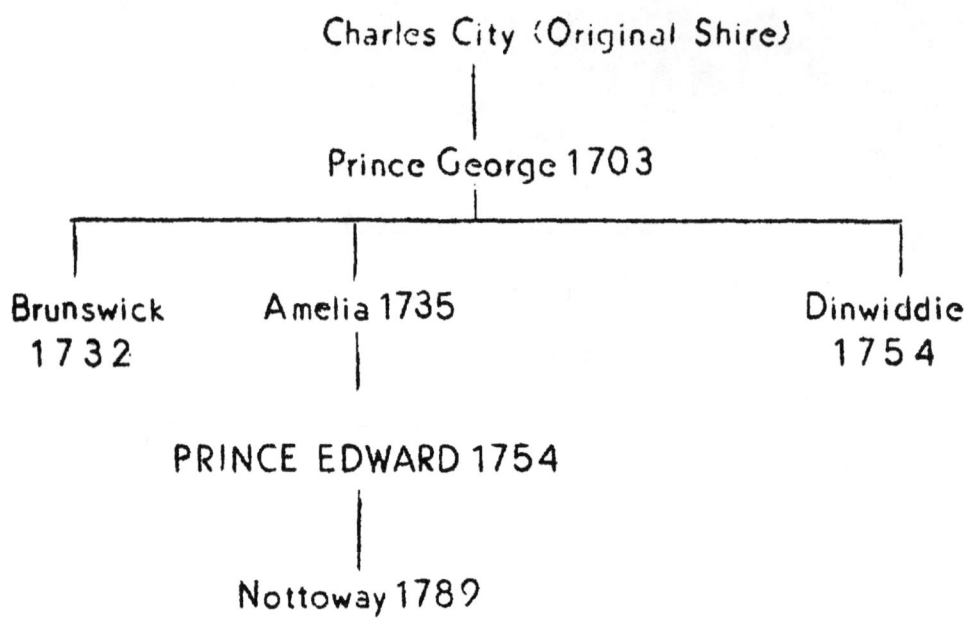

Preface

Mrs. L.L. Chapman of Smithfield, Virginia, and Mrs. H. A. Knorr of Pine Bluff, Arkansas, have issued, in attractive form, the "Marriages of Southampton County, Virginia, 1750-1800".

Mrs. Knorr now publishes a volume containing "The Marriages of Prince Edward County, Virginia" from 1754 (when the County was carved from Amelia) to 1810, - a very large number.

Mrs. Knorr asks me to say a word as to the importance of these marriage bonds or licenses.

As one who has done a considerable amount of genealogical research, I am in a position to know how wide spread is the interest in the records of Prince Edward. I have, in the past twenty-five years, received many hundreds of letters from forty states and from foreign countries making inquiries about ancestors, the majority of them connected with this county.

Fortunately the Prince Edward records, marriage licenses, will books, deed books and order books (Minutes of the Court) are in excellent condition and from day to day there are visitors from all over the United States seeking ancestral data at the Court House in Farmville. A special room with chairs and tables is provided.

<u>The marriage bonds (licenses) are the key to further information in the pursuit of ancestors.</u>

From Prince Edward have come officers and private soldiers in the French and Indian wars; two generals in the War of the Revolution and many lesser officers and soldiers; officers and soldiers in the War of 1812 and the Mexican War; one General and a larger number of other officers and soldiers in the war of 1861-1865. General Joseph E. Johnston, Commander of the Army of the Tennessee was a native of Prince Edward. So were Major R. L. Dabney, Chief of Staff to General Stonewall Jackson; Andrew Reid Venable, inspector General and on the staff of General J. E. B. Stuart; Colonel Charles Scott Venable was on the staff of General Robert E. Lee.

Eight governors of Virginia and other states are to her credit; Judges of State Supreme Court; one United States Senator and one member of the Cabinet; dozens of authors in the fields of literature, the Church, education and medicine. One of her sons was Dr. J. P. Mettauer, a pioneer in surgery and of national reputation. To the pulpit of the various denominations she has furnished her share of the great.

Members of Constitutional Conventions in Virginia and in other states have been conspicuous; Presidents of Colleges, likewise. In the 1830's and 1840's at old Prince Edward Court House (now Worsham) was the celebrated Young Ladies Seminary with over 200 pupils. Hampden-Sydney College was established in 1885; Longwood College for Women was opened in 1884 and the Presbyterian Seminary for Men in 1823.

Surely Prince Edward takes a high place among her sister Counties of Virginia.

Mrs. Knorr is to be commended for her present publication.

Hampden-Sydney, Virginia
April 18, 1950

Foreword

No volume of the Marriages of Prince Edward County could have been possible without two superb genealogists - that grand old scholar, Dr. Joseph D. Eggleston and that pattern of generosity, Mrs. William S. Morton.

Long ago Dr. Eggleston made a transcription of the original bonds and no one without a thorough knowledge of Prince Edward names and people could have accurately read the old script.

Mrs. Morton copied the ministers' returns, a most laborious task as the ink was faded and the writing small and difficult to read. We owe them immeasurable gratitude.

Prince Edward was named for Edward Augustus, son of Frederick, Prince of Wales. In 1753 an Act was introduced to separate the present Prince Edward from Amelia, the establishment of the new county taking place in 1754 ("Virginia Counties" by Robinson p 189). The first minutes of the new county are recorded in the County Court Orders 1754-1758. John Le Neve served as the first Clerk from 1754 to 1783 then Francis Watkins succeeded him serving from 1783 to 1825. The first Court House was at the village of Worsham near the location of Hampden-Sydney College. Farmville, the present county seat was established 1798.

It gives me great pleasure to acknowledge here the courtesy of the County Clerk, Mr. Horace Adams and his assistants, Mrs. Robert B. Wilson and Mrs. Richard Tunstall. It was very pleasant working in their new, comfortable record room, knowing they were near at all times to call on if and when I needed help.

So, I give you Prince Edward Marriages. Dr. Eggleston sums up the importance of the marriages when he says "The marriage bonds are the key to further information in the pursuit of ancestors." This volume contains the marriage bonds and the ministers' returns, an aggregate of 1303 entries.

Here is one of the keys!

Catherine Lindsay Knorr

Mrs. H. A. Knorr
1401 Linden Street
Pine Bluff, Arkansas

MARRIAGES OF PRINCE EDWARD COUNTY, VIRGINIA - 1754-1810

2 November 1755.   and   Morris. John Morris gives his consent for his dau. to marry. Wit. Joseph and Martha Ward.

27 March 1807. James ADAMS and Sarah Chumley, dau. of John Chumley. Sur. James Ewing, Jr. James is son of Robert Adams.

2 March 1791. Henry ADKERSON and Betsy Howel. Minister's returns. See Henry Atkinson.

1785. Edmund AIRS and Maxey or Massey Bidditt.

21 December 1772. Archer ALLEN and Elizabeth Allen, dau. of James Allen who is surety.

24 April 1777. Benjamin ALLEN and Cussias Chambers, dau. of Josiah Chambers. Sur. Charles Allen, Jr.

29 January 1781. Benjamin ALLEN and Elizabeth Hudson, age 21, dau. of Charles Hudson who is sur. Consent of Susannah Hudson. Married 8 February.

24 April 1777. Charles ALLEN, Jr. and Elizabeth Chambers, dau. of Josiah Chambers who consents.

12 January 1801. James ALLEN and Peggy Calhoon, dau. of Adam Calhoon, deceased. Sur. Adam Calhoon.

17 October 1808. John C. ALLEN and Nancy Watson, dau. of Samuel Watson.

17 August 1778. Nathaniel ALLEN and Pamala Hudson. Sur. Peter Puckett.

11 December 1804. Samuel ALLEN, Jr. and Mary W. Walker, dau. of William T. Walker who is surety. Married 13 Dec.

14 December 1804. Samuel V. ALLEN and Peggy Stewart, dau. of Nevin Stewart who consents. Sur. Harry E. Watkins. Married 15 December.

21 April 1807. William A. ALLEN and Susannah P. Manning, dau. of Nathaniel Manning, deceased. Consent of her guardian, Paul Carrington. Sur. Benjamin Watkins. Married 23 April. (See History of Halifax, p. 347.)

16 October 1804. Pleasant AMOS and Elizabeth Kerr Johnson, dau. of John Johnson who is surety.

19 September 1785. David ANDERSON and Lucy Horsley, dau. of William Horsley, deceased. Sur. Christopher Holland. Married 21 September. Lucy Husby in Minister's returns.

17 September 1792. Larkin ANDERSON and Elizabeth McGehee, dau. of Jacob McGehee who consents. Sur. Benjamin Hodnett.

21 December 1795. Larkin ANDERSON and Polly Carter. Sur. Robert Anderson. Married 31 December.

19 May 1800. Larkin ANDERSON and Elizabeth Hines, dau. of William Hines who is surety. Minister's returns say married May 1806.

19 June 1809. Larkin ANDERSON and Judith T. Foster, dau. of Richard Foster, Sr. Sur. Peter Johnston. Married 21 June.

19 April 1790. Robert ANDERSON and Mildred Carter, widow of Waddle Carter. Sur. James Wade, Jr.

29 April 1778. Thomas ANDERSON and Sarah Weldon Anderson, dau. of Francis Anderson, Sr. who consents and states neither of the contracting parties are of Prince Edward. Sur. Thomas Lorton.

26 July 1805. Thomas ANDERSON and Judith Taylor, dau. of Joseph Taylor who consents. Sur. Blake B. Woodson.

1 February 1774. William ANDERSON and Mary Holcomb, dau. of Philemon Holcomb who is surety.

23 November 1807. William ANDERSON and Mary V. Martin, dau. of Robert Martin. Sur. Charles Venable, Jr.

21 November 1783. Aken ARMES and Molly Waddill. Waddell in Minister's returns.

12 August 1797. Micajah ARMES and Judith Hill, dau. of John Hill who is surety. Married 22 August.

30 October 1809. William ARMES and Mary W. Forrest, dau. of Abraham Forrest, deceased. Sur. Josiah Forrest. Married 2 November.

11 April 1788. John ARMISTEAD and Mary Ann Spencer, dau. of Sharp Spencer who is surety. John Armistead of Cumberland Co. Married 15 April.

17 January 1797. Thomas ARMSTRONG and Amelia Cason, dau. of Seth Cason who consents. Sur. John Cason.

24 March 1790. David ARNOLD and Patience Harris, dau. of Lewis Harris, deceased, and Elizabeth Harris. David son of John Arnold. Sur. Edward Harris.

13 December 1784. John ARNOLD, Jr. and Mary Cason, dau. of Seth Cason who consents. Sur. Joseph Adcock. John son of John Arnold Sr.

23 March 1803. Wyatt ARNOLD and Keziah Penick, dau. of William and Judith Penick. Married 24 March.

4 December 1784. Zachariah ARNOLD and Nancy Beasley, dau. of John Beasley, deceased. Guardian John Johns consents. Sur. Moses Arnold. Married February 1785.

8 January 1800. Alexander ASKEW and Rhoda Guill, dau. of Alexander Guill who consents. Sur Barnett Brightwell.

24 February 1779. William ASCHEW and Elizabeth Robinson. Sur. Isaac Robinson.

26 July 1779. Joel ASHLEY and Violet Caldwell. Sur. Paul Caldwell.

28 February 1791. Henry ATKINSON and Betsy Howell. Sur. Edmond Fears. Married 2 March. See Henry Adkerson.

1 June 1801. John ATKINSON and Elizabeth Smith, dau. of John Smith who is surety. Married 4 June.

27 May 1793. Spencer ATKINSON and Frances Estes, dau. of Henry Estes who consents. Sur. Henry Estes, Jr.

19 December 1796 (1795?). John ATWELL, Jr. and Patsy Rice, dau. of Joseph Rice. Sur. John Atwell, Sr. Married 22 February 1796.

21 February 1785. Edmund AVIS and Biddeth Maxey. Sur. Thomas Gibson.

11 October 1809. George BACKUS and Dolly Chapple (Born 4 July 1787), dau. of Samuel Chapple, deceased. Sur. Jack Vaughan. Married 14 October.

20 January 1810. Daniel BAGBY and Patsy Mosely, dau. of Robert Mosely who consents. Sur. James Bagby. Married 24 January. Minister's returns say Betsy Mosby.

7 January 1799. George BAGBY and Polly Neal, dau. of Stephen Neal, deceased. Sur. Henry Anderson. Married 12 June 1799.

21 June 1784. James BAGBEY and Patsey Price. Sur. Charles Price. Married 20 December. See James Bagby.

20 December 1784. James BAGBY and Patsy Price. Minister's returns.

16 November 1795. Jesse BAGBY and   . Sur. John Woodfin.

30 July 1788. Robert BAGBY and Betsy Penick, dau. of William Penick who is surety. Robert Bagby of Buckingham Co. (Betsy dau. of William & Judith (Pate?) Penick.)

20 March 1795. William BAGBY and Nancy Hubbard, dau. of John Hubbard. Sur. John Bagby. Married 26 March.

7 January 1799. George BAGLEY and Polly Neal, dau. of Stephen Neal, deceased. Sur. Henry Anderson. Married 12 Jan.

13 August 1800. William BAILEY and Prudence Ellington, dau. of Hezekiah Ellington, deceased. Guardian, Ridley Ellington consents. Married 14 August.

17 June 1799. Andrew BAKER, Jr. and Polly Price, dau. of William Price, Jr. who is surety. Married 19 June.

13 February 1795. Blake BAKER and Nancy Allen, widow of Daniel Allen. Sur. William Cowan. Married 14 February.

18 March 1782. Caleb BAKER and Jane Thompson. Sur. John Black. Married 27 March.

21 December 1801 (1807?). Elliott BAKER and Kizzey Brown, dau. of Wilson Brown, deceased. Sur. William Scott.

1 September 1802. John BAKER and Nancy Baldwin, dau. of William Baldwin who is surety. Married 15 September.

14 May 1784. Caleb BALDWIN and Mary Hill, dau. of John Hill who consents. Sur. Temple Davis.

16 December 1799. Charles BALDWIN and Polly Walker Penick, dau. of William and Judith Penick. Sur. William Penick. Married 19 December.

15 October 1791. John BALDWIN and Sally Davidson, dau. of Joshua Davidson, deceased. Consent of her mother, Sarah Davidson. Married 20 October by Rev. Robert Foster.

20 October 1791. John BALDWIN and Sally Davis. By Robert Foster. Evidently same as above.

24 February 1794. John BALDWIN, Jr. and Annie Simmons, dau. of John Simmons. Sur. John Baldwin Sr., Married 27 February.

21 December 1801 (1807?). John BALDWIN and Nancy Akin, dau. of Charles Akin, deceased. Sur. Josiah Perkinson.

1785. Samuel BALDWIN and Mary Griffin, dau. of William Griffin who consents. Sur. William Baldwin.

16 September 1799. Samuel BALDWIN and Polly Womack, dau. of William Womack, Sr., Sur. William Womack.

27 May 1778. William BALDWIN and Mary Griffin, widow of James Griffin, Sur. James Roberts.

25 March 1782. William BALDWIN and Eliza Baker. Marriage Register. See William Baulding.

20 December 1779. Thomas BALEY and Milley Clark, dau. of John Clark who is surety. (Mildred C. Clark.)

27 January 1800. Daniel BARKSDALE and Polly Watson, dau. of John Watson, Sr. who consents. Sur. John Watson, Jr.

November 1763. Joseph BARKSDALE and Hannah Butler. Sur. Charles Yancy.

15 March 1784. Jacob BARNES and Susanna North. Sur. William North.

30 January 1783. John BARNETT and Mary Carter. Marriage Register.

22 August 1782. Benjamin BARTLETT and Alee Evans. Marriage Register.

6 August 1789. Lodowick BASEBEACH and Sally Day, dau. of Richard Day, deceased. Sur. Edward Farley. Lodowick Basebeach son of Lucretia Basebeach.

20 November 1795. Pears BASEBEACH and Tabby Chapman, widow of Stephen Chapman. Sur. Roberson C. Day. Married 22 Nov.

21 January 1793. John BASS and Betsy Wade, dau. of Charles Wade. Sur. James Wade.

26 February 1806. Roling BASS and Martha Walthall, dau. of Thomas Walthall who is surety. Married 27 February. Rolling Bass in Register.

27 February 1806. Rolling BASS and Martha Walthall. Minister's returns. See Roling Bass.

30 December 1800. Bartlett BAUGH and Nancy Woodridge, dau. of Simon Woodridge who consents. Sur. Thomas Franklin. Married 2 January 1801. Wooldridge in Minister's returns.

27 January 1808. Peyton BAUGHAN and Polly Waddell, dau. of William Waddell who consents and is surety.

25 March 1782. William BAULDING and Elizabeth Baker. Minister's returns. See William Baldwin.

4 May 1792. James BAVEN and Betsy Green. Marriage Register.

16 December 1786. Thomas BEADEL and Priscilla Osborne, dau. of Thomas Osborne. Sur. Thomas Beadel of Amelia Co. Drucilla in will - pencil note.

17 September 1804. John BEAN and Elizabeth Dodd, dau. of Nicholas Dodd, deceased. Sur. John Rudd.

6 October 1792. Fuqua BEASLEY and Rachel Hurt, dau. of Benjamin Hurt who consents. Sur. Obadiah Hurt.

17 December 1798. Hiram BEASLEY and Elizabeth Fore, dau. of Joseph Fore who consents. Sur. John Fore.

4 November 1801. Oswell BEAVERS and Jane Archer Owen, dau. of William and Mary Owen. See Oswell Bevis.

24 December 1798. Hiram BEAZLEY and Elizabeth Fore. Minister's returns.

19 November 1804. David BELL and Elizabeth Davis, dau. of Nicholas Davis who is surety.

20 December 1773. George BELL and Rebecca Calhoon, dau. of Adam Calhoon who consents. Sur. James Carter.

19 January 1807. George W. BELL and Lucy S. Bigger, dau. of Tommy Bigger. Sur. James Bigger.

21 August 1788. James BELL and Betsy Richards, dau. of John Richards who consents. Sur. Joseph Bell of Prince Edward Co. James Bell of Buckingham Co.; son of Thomas Bell.

11 January 1802. James BELL and Mary Allen, dau. of James Allen who is surety.

17 December 1807. Southy BELL and Mary Lewis, dau. of Pleasants Lewis who is surety. Married 1 January 1808.

20 November 1797. Elisha BENNETT and Lucy Cason, dau. of Seth Cason who consents. Elisha son of William Bennett who consents. Sur. Philip Chapman. Married 29 November.

26 November 1785. John BENNETT and Judith Hubbard, dau. of John Hubbard who consents. Sur. John Fielder.

10 March 1787. John BENNETT and Sally Clarke, dau. of John Clarke who consents. Sur. John Clarke, Jr. Married 13 March.

26 October 1796. William BENNETT and Sarah Graham, dau. of James Graham who is surety.

4 January 1794. Peter BERRY and Elizabeth Robins, dau. of William Robins. Sur. Benoni Overstreet.

25 April 1810. Joseph BERRY, Jr. and Sibbeller Ellington, dau. of William Ellington who consents. Sur. Thomas Ellington. Married 27 April.

13 April 1793. Thomas BERRY and Mary Hawkins, dau. of Philip Hawkins who consents. Sur. Josiah Sharp. Married 18 April.

4 August 1800. Thomas BERRY and Lucy Berry, dau. of Joseph Berry Sr. Sur. Joseph Berry, Jr.

27 June 1787. Elisha BETTS and Sally Walton, dau. of George Walton who consents. Sur. Stephen Davis. Minister's returns say married December 1787.

15 February 1808. Spencer BETTS and Betsy Burke, widow of Richard F. Burke. Sur. Dabney Morris.

4 November 1801. Oswell BEVIS and Jane Owen, dau. of William Owen who consents. Sur. William Baldwin. See Oswell Beavers.

22 February 1790. John BIBB and Lucy Jane Lockett, dau. of Stephen Lockett who consents. Sur. Osborn Lockett.

26 September 1773. Richard BIBB and Lucy Booker, dau. of Edward Booker. Sur. William Bibb.

4 December 1779. Capt. William BIBB and Sally Wiatt of New Kent. Bibb of Prince Edward Co. Personal Notices from the Virginia Gazette

6 July 1791. Richard BILLUPS and Elizabeth Redd, dau. of Thomas Redd who consents. Sur. Thomas Redd, Jr. Richard Billups of Lunenburg Co.

23 February 1801. Joseph BINFORD and Mary Sneed Le Grand, dau. of Alexander Le Grande who is surety. Nancy Sneed Le Grand in Minister's returns.

31 May 1796. Lee BIRD and Polly Caldwell, dau. of Henry Caldwell who consents. Sur. Allen Caldwell. See Lee Byrd.

30 September 1809. Peter BLAND and Martha Wallace Nash, dau. of John Nash. Sur. Francis Nash.

13 July 1791. Abel BLANKENSHIP and Ann Carter, dau. of William Carter Sr., who consents. Sur. William Carter, Jr.

18 October 1802. James BLANTON and Elizabeth Williamson, dau. of Thomas Williamson, who is surety.

2 October 1807. John BLANTON and Sarah Davidson, dau. of William Davidson who consents. Sur. Abner Davidson. Married 8 October.

31 October 1795. Richard BLANTON and Jane Rice, dau. of James Rice who is surety.

8 June 1796. John BOATRIGHT and Jerusha Penick, dau. of William and Judith Penick. Sur. William Penick, Married 9 June.

26 July 1785. Reuben BOATRIGHT and Lucy Penick, dau. of William Penick who is surety. (Lucy dau. William and Judith (Pate?) Penick.)

29 September 1806. Daniel BOAZ and Frances Hix, widow of John Hix. Sur. James Hix. Married 2 October. See Daniel Boze.

18 November 1805. Meshack BOAZ and Nancy Penick, dau. of Charles Penick, deceased and Agnes (Clark) Penick. Sur. Robert Penick (brother). Married 21 November.

11 July 1786. John BOISSEAU and Nancy Carter, dau. of Waddle Carter, deceased. Sur. Samuel Carter. Married 15 July. See John Bossieau.

14 November 1805. Stith BOLLING and Eliza Perkinson, dau. of John Perkinson who consents. Sur. James J. Foster. Married 20 November. See Stith Bowling.

8 August 1809. Edmund BOOKER and Elizabeth R. Foster, dau. of Robert Foster, deceased. Sur. James J. Foster. Married 10 August by Rev. John Bland.

6 July 1787. Davis BOOKER and Nancy Bibb, dau. of William Bibb who is surety. Minister's returns say married December 1787. By Rev. John A. Smith.

4 June 1794. George BOOKER and Susannah Cunningham. Sur. Peter Le Grand. Married 6 June.

6 November 1810. George W. BOOKER and Lucy Gillespie, dau. of William Gillespie, deceased. Guardian James Gillespie consents and is surety. G. Booker consents for George W. Booker, his son.

7 February 1781. John BOOKER and Mary Booker. Married by Rev. James B. Smith. Marriage Register.

19 November 1804. Edmund BORUM and Nancy McGehee, dau. of Abraham McGehee who is surety. Married 6 December.

8 December 1806. Jacob BORUM and Elizabeth Tyree, dau. of William Tyree who consents. Sur. Philander Tyree. Married 9 December.

19 December 1804. James BORUM and Patsy Tucker, dau. of Joseph Tucker who is surety. Married 22 December.

15 July 1799. William BORUM and Elizabeth Ellington, dau. of Hezekiah Ellington, deceased. Sur. James Hudson. Married 23 July.

15 July 1786. John BOSSIEAU and Nancy Carter. Minister's returns. See John Boisseau.

7 January 1807. John BOULTON and Mary Russell, dau. of Joseph Russell who consents. Sur. Robert Boulton.

2 May 1792. James BOWERS and Betsy Greer (sic), dau. of Malachi Green who is surety. Married 4 May.

20 November 1805. Stith BOWLING and Eliza Perkinson. Minister's returns. See Stith Bolling.

8 November 1788. John Sutton BOWMAN, Jr. and Phoebe Owen, dau. of Jesse and Ann Owen who consent. Sur. William Ligon. Married 5 December.

18 May 1756. Royal BOWMAN and Elizabeth Morton, dau. of Thomas Morton who consents. Sur. Thomas Turpin.

21 November 1791. Sutton BOWMAN and Mary Frazer, dau. of Alexander Frazer who consents. Sur. Richard Blanton. Married 30 December.

2 October 1806. Daniel BÓZE and Frances Hix. Minister's returns. See Daniel Boaz.

20 November 1781. John BRACKETT and Phebe Davidson. Sur. Joshua Davidson. Married 20 November.

14 December 1796. John BRACKETT and Sally P. Anyan, dau. of John Anyan, deceased. Sur. John Watson. Married 15 Dec.

29 March 1786. William BRADBURY and Winnie Hines, dau. of William and Sarah Hines who consent. Sur. Thomas Collier.

9 January 1788. William BRADBURY and Mary Smith, widow of James Smith. Sur. William Ellington. Married 10 January.

2 May 1781. Edward BRADLEY and Catherine Morain (?) Sur. Ezekiel Hendrick.

19 September 1785. Benjamin BRADSHAW and Mary Rowlett, dau. of John and Edith Rowlett who consent. Sur. John Penick, Jr. Married 13 October.

7 September 1791. Mathew BRANCH and Elizabeth Hamblen, widow of John Hamblen. Sur. J. Hamblen.

11 February 1802. William BRANCH and Elizabeth B. Worsham, dau. of William Worsham who is surety. Married 2 February.

3 December 1790. William W. BREEDLOVE and Sarah H. Foster, dau. of Richard Foster who consents. Sur. Samuel Foster. Married 30 December.

17 March 1807. Alexander BRIDGLAND and Harriet Susannah Thornton, dau. Sterling Thornton who is surety.

3 August 1807. Alexander BRIGHTWELL and Sally Carter, dau. of Joseph Carter. Sur. John W. Lumpkin. Married 6 August.

14 December 1786. Anderson BRIGHTWELL and Nancy Brightwell, dau. of Runald Brightwell who consents for both. Sur. Barnett Brightwell. Reynolds Brightwell in will.

21 February 1782. Barnett BRIGHTWELL and Mary Guill. Marriage Register.

25 April 1803. Samuel BRIGHTWELL and Betsy A. Moore, dau. of Pleasants Moore, deceased.

25 April 1803. Samuel BRIGHTWELL and Betsy A. Moon, dau. of Pleasants Moon, deceased. Evidently the same people.

5 December 1804. William BRIGHTWELL and Nancy Brightwell, dau. Barnett Brightwell who consents. Sur. Samuel Shepard. Married 6 December.

30 December 1800. William BRIGHTWELL and Mary Young, dau. of Henry Young, deceased. Sur. Barnett Brightwell.

6 May 1809. Boller BRIZENDINE and Sally Hill, dau. of William Hill who is surety.

14 January 1800. John BROADWAY and Nancy Davison, dau. of John Davison who consents and is surety. Married 16 January. Davidson in Minister's returns.

15 October 1791. Joseph BROADWAY and Elizabeth Davidson, dau. of Joshua Davidson, deceased, and Sarah Davidson who consents. Sur. George Davidson. Married 20 October.

2 October 1804. Joseph BROADWAY and Elizabeth Roberts, dau. of Alexander Roberts who consents. Sur. John Baldwin.

3 March 1785. William BROADWAY and Sally Davidson. Marriage Register.

27 September 1788. Aaron BROOKS and Sarah Wood, dau. of James Wood who consents. Sur. Patrick Higgins. (Dau. of Joseph? Wood).

19 December 1799. Anthony BROOKS and Polly Bradshaw, dau. of John Bradshaw, deceased. Sur. Richard Bradshaw.

20 December 1802. Armistead (or Armstreet) BROOKS and Jennett Sherrow (?), dau. of John Hamblen (?), deceased. Sur. Daniel Hamblen. See Armsed Brooks.

23 December 1802. Armsed BROOKS and Jennett S. Hamblin. Minister's returns. See Armistead Brooks.

18 August 1788. Bartlett BROOKS and Susannah Smith, dau. of Henry Smith, deceased. Consent of Mary Smith. Also Thomas Brooks as to Bartlett Brooks. Sur. William Baldwin.

7 April 1787. David BROOKS and Sarah Brooks, dau. of George Brooks, deceased. Sur. John Frazer.

20 April 1795. David BROOKS and Frances Berryman, dau. of William Berryman, deceased. Sur. Robert Holt. Married 2 May. Minister's returns say Perryman.

15 September 1800. David BROOKS and Elizabeth Mattox, dau. of Henry Mattox, deceased. Sur. Henry Ligon.

16 November 1807. George BROOKS and Polly Kuling or Keeling, dau. William Kuling or Keeling who is surety. Keeling in Register.

21 March 1791. Hezekiah BROOKS and Nancy Smith. Sur. William Baldwin.

31 May 1785. James BROOKS and Ann Wood. Sur. Joseph Wood.

5 October 1795. Jesse BROOKS and Mary Vaughan, dau. of Thomas Vaughan who consents and is surety. Married 8 Oct.

20 February 1792. John BROOKS and Milley Perryman, dau. of William Perryman, deceased. Sur. William Baldwin. Married 23 March.

4 December 1804. Frederick BROWN and Mary Robertson, dau. of Jesse Robertson who is surety. Married 6 December.

4 March 1795. Byrd BROWN and Mary Goode, dau. of Robert Goode, deceased. Sur. Samuel Goode. Byrd Brown of Campbell Co.

10 December 1787. James BROWN and Patty Venable, dau. of Charles Venable who consents. Sur. Robert Martin.

12 May 1756. John C. BROWN and Elizabeth Atkins. Sur. W. Brown.

14 March 1785. Alexander BRUCE and Ann Penick. Sur. Thomas Penick. Married 15 March. Dau. of John and Mary (Mallory) Penick.

13 August 1782. Jesse BRYANT and Mary Hill Nelson, dau. of Henry Nelson who consents and is surety. Married 14 August.

4 January 1792. Patterson BULLOCK and Rhoda Watkins, widow of Joel Watkins. Sur. Philip Watkins. Married 5 January.

7 January 1796. Richard F. BURKE and Betsy Perkinson, dau. of John Perkinson. Sur. Dabney Morris. Married 12 January by Rev. John Cameron.

16 September 1797. Richard BURKE and Frances Dunnivant, widow of Clement Dunnivant. Sur. Tapley Akin. Married 17 September. See Richard Burks.

16 December 1805. James BURKS and Polly Owen, dau. of William Owen. Sur. Alexander Marshall. (Polly dau. of William and Mary Owen.)

12 January 1796. Richard F. BURKS and Betsy Perkerson. By Rev. John Cameron.

17 September 1797. Richard BURKS and Frances Dunnivant. Minister's returns. See Richard Burke.

31 October 1782. Thompson BURKS and Anne Rice. Marriage Register.

18 June 1798. William BURKS and Aggathy Owens, dau. of Jesse Owen. Sur. John S. Bowman. Married 29 June.

31 October 1797 (1799?). John BURTON and Elizabeth Rutledge dau. of Thomas Rutledge who consents. Sur. William Redd. Married 4 November.

18 December 1797. Samuel BUTLER and Naomi Childress, dau. Reps. Childress who consents. Sur. Zach. Rice. Married 22 December.

2 June 1796. Lee BYRD and Mary Caldwell. Minister's returns. See Lee Bird.

20 October 1803. Nicholas CABELL, Jr. and Peggy R. Venable, dau. of Samuel W. Venable. Sur. Benjamin Watkins.

2 May 1766. Henry CALDWELL and Martha Allen, dau. of Malcum Allen. Sur. Robert Bird.

16 April 1804. Thomas CALDWELL and Betsy Wilkerson, dau. of Lovel and Sally Wilkerson who consent. Sur. George Wilkerson.

8 December 1799. Adam CALHOON and Jane Daniel, dau. of John Daniel who is surety.

10 September 1806. James CALHOON and Hannah Watson, dau. of Drury Watson. Sur. Humphrey Nelson.

25 January 1796. George CARDWELL and Ann Hamilton, dau. of Alexander Hamilton, deceased. Consent of Mother Elizabeth Hamilton. Sur. Alexander Hamilton. Married 26 Jan.

17 February 1783. John CARROL and Lucrecy Huskerson. Minister's returns. See John Cassell.

3 October 1782. Thomas CARSON and Anne Porter. Marriage Register.

13 October 1807. Elias E. CARTER and Prudence Bailey, widow of William Bailey. Sur. Jesse Ellington. Married 15 October.

15 April 1806. John CARTER and Polly Bigger, dau. of James Bigger. Sur. Joseph Bigger.

29 December 1772. Richard CARTER and Susanna Bigger. Sur. John Bigger, Jr.

9 January 1798. Samuel CARTER and Elizabeth McRobert, dau. of Archibald McRobert who is surety. Married 11 Jan.

16 April 1764. Theodrick CARTER, Jr. and Judith Cunningham. Sur. Alexander Cunningham.

21 May 1764. Thomas CARTER and Sarah Martin. Sur. Thomas Scott.

19 December 1803. William CARTER, Jr. and Lucy Wootton, dau. of William Wootton. Sur. John Redd. Married 22 Dec.

15 June 1794. Edward CARY and Susanna Leneave. Marriage Register. See Edward Casey.

10 November 1788. Harwood CARY and Mary Cardwell, dau. of John Cardwell who consents. Sur. Willshire Cardwell.

8 February 1774. William CARY and Mary Booker, widow of Booker of Amelia Co. Sur. John Bigger, Jr.

26 April 1793. William Haynes CARY and Lucy Cardwell, dau. of John Cardwell who consents. Sur. George Cardwell, Jr. Married 28 April.

15 June 1794. Edward CASEY and Susannah Leneave. Marriage register. See Edward Cary.

30 October 1798. Seth CASON and Judith Hurt, widow of Benjamin Hurt, and Dau. of Abraham Ferris. Sur. David Thaxton. Married 2 November.

17 February 1783. John CASSELL(?). and Luc. Huskerson. Marriage Register. See John Carrol.

21 April 1794. William CAVENDER and Dicey Bryant, dau. of Jesse Bryant. Sur. John Bryant.

18 December 1778. Isham CHAFFIN and Betsy Bird. Sur. Williamson Bird.

31 March 1764. John CHAMBERS and Rhoda Watkins. Sur. Richard Holland. Own consent. John Chambers of Buckingham Co.

27 October 1797. Philip CHAPMAN and Polly Bennett, dau. of William Bennett who consents. Sur. Carter Thompson. Married 31 October.

13 December 1784. Jesse CHAPPEL and Martha Baldwin, dau. of Thomas Baldwin who consents. Sur. Caleb Baldwin. Married 20 December. See Jesse Chapple.

7 July 1789. John CHAPPELL and Mary Ann Hays. Sur. Samuel White.

20 December 1784. Jesse CHAPPLE and Martha Baulding. Minister's returns. See Jesse Chappel.

30 November 1781. Charles CHATRALL and Frances Rice. Marriage Register.

17 September 1796. James CHILDRESS and Mary Carr, dau. of Ann Carr and Hugh Carr, deceased. Sur. Obadiah Woodson. Married 28 September.

19 November 1781. Robert CHILDRESS and Rachel Estes. Sur. Abraham Estes. Married 6 December. Marriage Register says Rachel Easter.

18 February 1804. William CHILDRESS and Phoebe Hill, dau. of William Hill who is surety.

16 October 1809. James CHUMLEY and Martha Adams, dau. of Robin Adams, deceased. Sur. John Chumley.

5 February 1806. John CHUMLEY and Palethia Adams, dau. of Robin Adams, deceased. Sur. William T. Walker. Register says Palthria. Minister's returns say Patthrea.

15 February 1796. Robert CHUMNEY and Fanny Sadler, dau. of John Sadler who is surety.

15 December 1788. Jonias CLAIBORNE and Elizabeth Tanner, dau. of Joseph Tanner, deceased. Sur. Thomas Tanner.

16 December 1805. John CLARK, Jr. and Elizabeth Redd, dau. of John Redd who is surety.

18 April 1808. Norry CLARK and Martha Cody, dau. of Edmund Cody, deceased. Sur. John L. Cody.

7 September 1790. Mathew CLARK and Abigail Baldwin, dau. of Thomas Baldwin who consents. Sur. Caleb Baldwin.

17 March 1788. John CLARKE and Susanna   . Sur. Thomas Robertson. (She married 2nd Royall Lockett 1797.)

14 December 1791. Richard CLARKE and Susannah Elizabeth Scott, widow of John Scott. Wit. F. Watkins. Sur. George Booker.

7 September 1790. Matthew CLARKE and Abegail Boulding. Sur. Caleb Boulding. Wit. Richard Watkins. Bond signed Caleb Baldwin.

21 February 1803. Foushee CLAUGHTON and Prudence Hudson, widow of James Hudson. Sur. John L. Cralle. Richard Claughton consents for his son Foushee Claughton.

10 February 1804. Isham CLEMENT and Sally Redd or Rudd, dau. of John Redd or Rudd, who is surety. Married 24 Feb.

19 December 1785. Charles Rice COBBS and Mary North, dau. of William North who is surety.

12 October 1809. Thomas COBBS, Jr. and Sarah Tredway, dau. of Moses Tredway, deceased. Sur. Moses Tredway. Thomas son of Thomas Cobbs, Sr. of Buckingham County.

12 September 1782. Anderson COCKE and Betsy Michaux. Marriage Register.

5 December 1797. Richard COCKE and Polly Watkins, dau. of Henry Watkins. Sur. Thomas Walton. Married 6 December.

14 November 1797. John COCKRAHAM and Sarah Hamblen, dau. of John Hamblen, deceased. Sur. William Hamblen.

20 July 1791. Abner COFFEE and Christiana Kelly, dau. of John Kelly who consents. Sur. James Wooldridge. Married 21 July.

4 November 1801. Daniel (David?) COFFEE and Sythe Meadows, Marriage Register.

30 August 1806. Pleasant COFFEE and Judith Meadows, dau. of Joel and Mary Meadows. Sur. Isaac Meadows. Married 6 September.

24 December 1802. Francis COLE and Martha Clibourn, dau. of George Clibourn. Sur. Thomas Clibourn. Married 25 Dec.

20 September 1797. James D. COLE and Sarah Malloy, widow of Thomas Malloy. Sur. George Moore. Married 27 September.

10 October 1804. Henry COLEMAN and Ann B. Oliver, dau. of Isaac Oliver, deceased. Sur. Elisha Betts.

6 April 1792. James COLEMAN and Peggy Cawthorn, widow of John Cawthorn. Sur. John Hubbard, married 9 April.

1 April 1805. James COLEMAN and Judith Cason, widow of Seth Cason. Sur. John Cook. Married 20 April.

17 December 1792. Stephen COLEMAN and Mary Fore, dau. of Joseph Fore who is surety. Stephen Coleman of Buckingham County.

8 February 1798. Benjamin COLLIER and Mary Collier, widow of Charles Collier. Sur. William Whitworth. Married 22 February. Recorded in Order Book Sept. 1798. Contract.

23 February 1784. Charles COLLIER, and Mary Whitworth, dau. of William Whitworth who consents. Sur. G. Walker. Married 24 February.

30 September 1765. John COLLIER and Hannah Hamlett. Sur. James Hamlett.

29 October 1789. Thomas COLLIER and Polly Carter, dau. of William Carter who consents. Sur. Thomas Fears. Married 30 October.

30 October 1783. William COLLINS and Martha Attwood. Marriage Register.

28 June 1809. Trent CONNER and Polly Gaulding, dau. of Richard Gaulding who is surety. Married 1 July.

17 January 1803. John COOK and Lucy Gray. Sur. William Gray.

17 October 1792. William COOK and Elizabeth Pettus, dau. of Stephen Pettus who is surety. Married 30 October.

6 March 1767. John COX and Tabitha Price, dau. of Pugh Price. Sur. Williamson Bird.

13 October 1797. John COX and Lucy Le Grand, dau. of Alexander Le Grand who is surety. Married 19 October.

31 December 1807. John COX and Sally Tuggle, dau. of John Tuggle who is surety.

10 March 1810. John C. CRADDOCK and Peggy R. Jackson, dau. of John Jackson who consents. Sur. Neil Jackson.

3 November 1810. Anderson CRAFTON and Mickey Fowlkes, dau. of Daniel Fowlkes who consents. Sur. James Fowlkes.

20 February 1805. Thomas T. CRAGHEAD and Frances E. Mathews, dau. of William Mathews, deceased. Sur. William T. Walker. Married 26 February.

20 August 1804. John L. CRALLE and Sally Dupuy, dau. of Stephen Dupuy who is surety.

11 March 1794. Joseph CRENSHAW and Martha Dawson, dau. of Henry Dawson, deceased. Sur. John Lundaman.

31 December 1795. Jonathan CRESAY and Sarah Berry, dau. of Joseph Berry who consents. Sur. John Piller.

20 November 1797. William CREWS and Phebe Penick, dau. of Thomas Penick who is surety. Phebe dau. of Thomas and Kesiah (Owen) Penick.

21 January 1771. Andrew CROCKETT and Sarah Ellitt. Sur. Robert Ellitt.

26 October 1763. Samuel CROCKETT and Jean Steel. Sur. Robert Steel. Samuel Crockett of Bedford County.

14 January 1760. William CROCKETT and Agnes Richie. Sur. Robert Hastie.

11 September 1809. Willis V. R. CRUTE and Susannah T. Watson, dau. of John Watson, Sr. who consents. Sur. Drury Watson. Married 12 September.

1 December 1796. Alexander CUNNINGHAM and Sarah Meadows, dau. of Jeremiah Meadows who is surety. Married 2 Dec.

5 April 1791. Andrew CUNNINGHAM and Martha Scott, dau. of Samuel Scott who consents. Sur. John Cunningham. Married 9 April.

31 January 1798. Jacob CUNNINGHAM and Lucy C. Walker. Sur. George Walker. Married 1 February.

27 September 1780. James CUNNINGHAM and Jane Daniel, widow. Sur. William Daniel. James Cunningham of Charlotte County.

10 February 1803. James CUNNINGHAM and Nancy Berry Davis, dau. of Littleberry Davis, deceased. Sur. Nathaniel Shepperson. Married 12 February.

8 February 1785. John CUNNINGHAM and Margaret Hill. Marriage Register.

26 July 1794. Richard CUNNINGHAM and Polly Johnson, dau. of William Johnson who consents. Sur. John Johnson. Married 1 August. Johnston in Register.

2 December 1807. Charles CURD and Nancy Lumpkin, dau. of Moore Lumpkin. Sur. John W. Lumpkin. "Ann Lumpkin, own consent."

20 June 1808. John DABNEY and Elizabeth Womack, dau. of Massanello Womack who consents. Sur. Robert V. Womack. Married 22 June.

2 February 1790. James DANIEL and Mary Parks, dau. of Joseph Parks who is surety.

18 November 1796. James DANIEL and Nancy Venable, dau. of Nathaniel Venable who consents. Sur. Joshua League. Married 19 November.

9 September 1805. James K. DANIEL and Violet Bell, dau. of George Bell who consents. Sur. John Bell.

17 November 1808. John C. DANIEL and Susan M. Watkins, dau. of Robert Watkins, deceased. Sur. Henry E. Watkins.

7 October 1801. Joseph DANIEL and Milly Nelson, dau. of Henry Nelson who is surety. Married 10 October.

12 September 1809. William T. DANIEL and Elizabeth Bell, dau. of George Bell who consents. Sur. William C. Bell. William S. Laniel in Register.

17 January 1788. William DARCUS and Mary Routledge. Minister's returns. See William Davis.

15 July 1805. James DAVENPORT and Judith Baker, dau. of Samuel Baker, deceased. Sur. John Baker. Married 18 July.

5 September 1800. Richard DAVENPORT and Jenny Baker, dau. of Douglas Baker, deceased. Sur. James Thompson.

19 November 1799. John DAVENPORT and Molly Baker, dau. of Samuel Baker who consents. Sur. John Baker. Married 21 November. John Davenport of Powhatan County.

21 December 1803. Abner DAVIDSON and Peggy Blanton, dau. of Richard Blanton, deceased, and Ellender Blanton who consents. Sur. John Davidson.

3 July 1795. Baker DAVIDSON and Betsey Womack dau. of William Womack, Sr. who consents. Sur. Tignal Womack. Married 8 July.

18 May 1756. George DAVIDSON and Sarah Atkins. Sur. William Atkins.

26 February 1799. George DAVIDSON and Elizabeth Blanton, dau. of Richard Blanton who consents. Sur. Joshua Blanton. Married 28 February.

4 December 1778. John DAVIDSON and Eleanor Ewing. Sur. Charles Penick.

21 January 1782. William DAVIDSON and Elizabeth Ewing. Sur. Williamson Bird.

1 September 1806. Joel DAVIS and Mary Shepperson, dau. of John Shepperson, deceased. Sur. James Hix. Married 2 Sept.

12 October 1780. Samuel DAVIS and Elizabeth Spencer. Marriage Register.

19 November 1770. Temple DAVIS and Ann Baldwin, dau. of William Baldwin who consents. Sur. William Davis. Temple Davis of Charlotte County.

5 January 1788. William DAVIS and Nancy Rutledge, dau. of Joseph Rutledge who is surety. See William Darcus.

20 December 1808. Thomas S. DAVIS and Mary Price, dau. of Joseph Price, deceased. Consent of her guardian Alexander Marshall. Consent of Samuel Davis for his son Thomas S. Davis. Sur. William H. Worsham.

6 August 1794. William DAVIS and Anne Hill, dau. of Davis Hill, deceased. William Davis son of Temple Davis who consents. Sur. Joel Maxcey.

21 December 1807. William DAVIS and Martha W. Venable, dau. of Robert Venable who consents. Sur. James Madison.

18 May 1756. George DAVISON and Sarah Atkins. Sur. William Atkins.

9 February 1790. George DAVISON and Creasey McDearmon, dau. of Dudley McDearmon who consents. Sur. John Brackett.

15 December 1789. John DAVISON and Nancy Rice, dau. of James Rice who is surety.

30 January 1792. Joseph DAVISON and Mary D. Broadway, dau. of Nicholas Broadway who is surety. Married 2 February.

13 July 1786. Joshua DAVISON and Mary McDearmon, dau. of Dudley McDearmon. Sur. William Collins. Married 26 Sept.

26 January   . William DAVISON and Elizabeth Ewing. Marriage Register.

26 October 1796. John DAY and Polly Sweeny, dau. of William Sweeny who consents. Sur. James Dixon. Married 27 October.

28 October 1779. Richard DEAN and Micha Williams, widow. Sur. Pugh Price.

1 August 1804. John DEATON and Elizabeth Forrest, dau. of Abraham Forrest who consents. Sur. Josiah Forrest.

18 November 1771. Francis DE GRAFFENREIDT and Molly Walton. Sur. George Walton.

11 January 1790. Bowler DEJARNETT and Keziah Wootten, dau. of William Wootten. Sur. Samuel Wootten.

20 January 1794. Richard DEJARNETT and Sarah Rowlett, dau. of Mackness Rowlett who is surety.

14 July 1795. Richard DENNIS and Elizabeth Haskins, dau. of Thomas Haskins who consents. Sur. Thomas Haskins, Jr.

16 December 1799. Nathan DEPRIEST and Nancy Foster, dau. of George Foster who is surety.

29 January 1810. John DESHAZER and Patience Ellington. Sur. Forrest Farley. Married 30 January.

9 January 1788. Benjamin DICKERSON and Sally Jennings, dau. of Elkannah and Sarah Jennings who consent. Sur. David Jennings.

18 August 1794. James DICKERSON and Polly Paris, dau. of James Paris. Sur. William Hill. (Or Patty Paris.)

19 November 1792. Nelson DICKERSON and Elizabeth Henderson, dau. of Daniel Henderson, deceased. Sur. David Jennings. Married 29 November.

8 May 1809. Williamson DICKERSON and Agnes O. Bennett, dau. of John Bennett. Sur. Littleberry Clark. Married 18 May. See William Dickinson.

18 May 1809. William DICKINSON and Agnes O. Bennett. Minister's returns. See Williamson Dickerson.

15 December 1806. Henry DILLON and Sally Clibourn, dau. of George Clibourn who consents. Sur. John Booth. Married 23 December. Marriage Register says Claiborn.

23 October 1796. John DILLON and Obedience Drinkard, widow of John Drinkard. Her father Reps. (?) Childress consents. Sur. Zachariah Rice.

19 October 1801. James DIXON and Patsey Meadows, dau. of James Meadows, deceased. Sur. John Dixon.

3 December 1802. William DODD and Sally Carter, dau. of William Carter, Sr., who is surety.

16 September 1805. John DODSON and Julia B. Rowlett, dau. of Mackness Rowlett who consents. Sur. Peter Rowlett. Married 12 November.

20 November 1798. Thomas DOSWELL and Elizabeth Walker, dau. of Benjamin Walker, deceased. Sur. James Vaughan.

25 December 1801. Thomas DOWDY and Nancy Boaz. Marriage Register.

25 July 1791. Francis DRINKARD and Martha Fleming. Sur. Beverley Fleming. Married 28 July. Marriage register says Martha Flanning.

18 November 1790. John DRINKARD and Obedience Childress, dau. of Reps. Childress who consents. Sur. Samuel Atwell.

12 February 1801. Ransome DUDLEY and Mary Anderson. Minister's returns.

2 March 1795. James DUNGEY and Elizabeth Fears, dau. of Absalom Fears who consents. Sur. John Smith. Married 5 Mar

23 November 1809. Daniel DUNNIVANT and Molly Rice, dau. of James Rice, deceased. Sur. John Blanton. Married 28 Nov.

1 December 1809. Henry G. DUPUY and Sarah Taylor, dau. of John Taylor, deceased. Sur. James Foster.

1782. James DUPUY and Mary Purnall. Marriage Register.

19 January 1810. Watkins DUPUY and Eliza S. Walton, dau. of John B. Walton who consents. Sur. Adam Bell. Married 23 January. Marriage register says Elizabeth J. Walton.

24 February 1804. Joel EARLY and Ave Andrews, dau. of John Andrews who is surety.

15 August 1807. Thomas J. EASTER and Polly Fowlkes. See Thomas A. Eastes.

15 August 1807. Thomas A. EASTES and Rossy Fowlkes, dau. of Josiah Fowlkes who is surety. Marriage Register says Easter also Polly Fowlkes. See Thomas J. Easter.

3 July 1807. Nicholas EDMUNDS and Janey Watkins Dupuy, dau. of John Dupuy who consents. Sur. Watkins Dupuy.

23 April 1800. Thomas ELDRIDGE and Patsey Miller, dau. of John Miller, deceased. Sur. John C. Miller.

6 January 1790. David ELLINGTON and Jane Harrison, dau. of William Harrison, deceased. Sur. Hezekiah Ellington. David Ellington of Lunenburg County.

13 September 1757 (1775?) Jeremiah ELLINGTON and Fanny Jones, age 21, dau. of Benjamin Jones. Sur. Adam Jones. Jeremiah son of David Ellington who consents.

27 May 1797. John ELLINGTON and Frances Waddell, dau. of Richard Waddell who consents. Sur. John Hutchinson. John son of Daniel Ellington who consents.

18 December 1809. John W. ELLINGTON and Sally C. Waddill, dau. of Dennis Waddill who consents. Sur. Forrest Farley. Marriage Register says Waddle.

24 November 1802. Joel ELLINGTON and Mary Webber. Marriage Register.

10 May 1799. Mourning ELLINGTON and Ritte Waddell, dau. of Jacob Waddell who consents. Sur. Joseph Farley.

15 June 1807. Pleasant ELLINGTON and Jenny Berry, dau. of Joseph Berry who is surety. Married 21 June. Marriage Register says Jane Berry.

11 February 1787. Andrew ELLIOTT and Nancy Womack, dau. of William Womack who consents. Sur. Abram Venable. Married 14 February.

15 November 1755. Archelaus ELMORE and Susanna Morris, dau. of John Morris who consents. Sur. Richard Childress.

30 December 1800. James EWING and Mary Venable, dau. of Jacob Venable. Sur. John Henderson.

23 September 1800. James EWING, Jr. and Rebecca Morgan, dau. of Thomas Morgan who is surety. Married 25 Sept.

2 January 1773. Samuel EWING and Mary Donald (Daniel?), Samuel son of George Ewing who consents and says Mary Daniel. Sur. John Martin.

4 September 1783. Samuel EWING and Diana Bird, dau. of Phileman Bird who consents. Sur. William Ewing.

21 October 1799. Lemuel FARGUSON and Sarah Hudson, dau. of John Hudson who consents. Sur. Thomas Hudson.

21 January 1761. Robert FARGUSON and Lydia Rice, dau. of Joseph Rice who consents. Sur. Philip Ryan. Robert Farguson son of Robert Farguson, Jr. now of Amelia Co.

27 April 1803. Benjamin FARIS and Susanna Morgan, dau. of Thomas Morgan who is surety. Married 30 April.

16 August 1792. Forrest FARLEY and Frances Ellington, dau. of John Ellington who is surety.

11 February 1804. Joseph FARLEY and Peggy Mason, dau. of Joseph Mason, deceased. Sur. James Vaughan.

18 April 1803. Lewellyn FARLEY and Phoebe Williamson, dau. of Robert Williamson, deceased. Sur. Pugh W. Price. Married 19 April.

10 August 1804. Stith FARLEY and Frances Goode, dau. of Robert Goode who consents. Sur. Joseph Goode.

24 September 1805. Charles FARMER and Sally Bell. Minister's returns. See Charles Farrar.

5 February 1801. Littleberry FARMER and Peggy Thaxton, dau. of David Thaxton who consents. Littleberry Farmer son of Forrest Farmer. Sur. Nathaniel Wilkerson. Married 13 February.

21 December 1802. Thomas FARMER and Nancy Dunnivant, dau. of Clement Dunnivant, deceased. Guardian, Stephen Dupuy consents. Sur. George Bagley.

3 September 1805. Charles FARRAR and Sally Bell, dau. of Stephen Bell, deceased. Sur. Southey Bell. Married 24 Sept. See Charles Farmer.

18 November 1799. Archibald FEARS and Nancy Shepperson, dau. of Walter Shepperson, deceased. Sur. John Taggart.

16 August 1791. Edmund FEARS and Sally Hood, dau. of James Hood who consents. Sur. John Hood. Married 10 Sept.

13 March 1789. John FEARS and Nancy Gallahorn, dau. of Charles Gallahorn who consents. Sur. Edmund Fears.

15 July 1805. William FEARS and Catherine Howell, dau. of John Howell. Sur. James Black. Married 18 July.

15 January 1807. Charles H. FEATHERSTON and Elizabeth Short Thornton, dau. of Sterling C. Thornton who consents. Sur. Cadwallader Jones.

18 January 1799. John FERRIS and Elizabeth Johnson, dau. of James Johnson who is surety.

19 January 1801. Archibald FERGUSON and Lucy Jennings, dau. of Allen Jennings who consents. Sur. Abner Coffee. Married 4 February.

1 September 1804. Jeffry FERGUSON and Rebecca Young, dau. of Henry Young. Sur. Obadiah Jenkins. Married 2 September.

18 November 1791. John FIELDER and Elizabeth Shephard, dau. of Robert Shephard of Goochland Co. who consents. Sur. John Thaxton.

15 July 1799. Robert FIELDER and Margaret Cawthorn, dau. of Thomas Cawthorn who is surety.

14 January 1797. Thomas FIELDER and Ruth Farmer, widow of Forrest Farmer. Sur. Andrew Christian. Married 19 January. Marriage register says Reitte Farmer.

17 May 1803. Charles FITCH and Judith W. Walker, dau. of William Walker, deceased. Sur. Alexander Le Grand.

13 September 1800. Samuel FITCH and Betsy W. Walker, dau. of William Walker, deceased. Sur. Washington Walker.

21 December 1778. Beverley FLEMING and Sally Waddell. Sur. Jacob Waddell.

13 July 1791. Robert FLEMING and Nancy Lewis, dau. of David Lewis who consents. Sur. Francis Drinkard, Jr. Married 15 July.

13 October 1797. Jesse FLIPPEN and Mildred Robinson, dau. of Jesse Robinson who is surety. Married 19 October. Marriage register says Robertson.

17 December 1778. Robert FLIPPEN and Mary Rice, her own consent. Sur. Stephen Lockett.

20 December 1781. Robert FLIPPEN and Mary Rice. Both dates given.

27 May 1793. Robert FLIPPEN and Elizabeth Dejarnett, dau. of John T. Dejarnett. See Josiah Cunningham.

20 December 1809. John FLOOD and Elizabeth D. Hudson, dau. of John Hudson. See Arthur Jones.

17 March 1766. Thomas FLOURNOY and Ann Martin. Sur. John Martin.

20 November 1803. David FLOWERS and Lucy Bowman, dau. of Thomas Bowman. Sur. William Goode.

16 January 1797. Francis Newton FORD and Sally Allen, dau. of Archer Allen who is surety. Married 19 January.

28 September 1802. Hezekiah FORD and Martha Brooks, dau. of Thomas Brooks, deceased. Sur. Arthur Connor. Marriage register says married 2 August.

12 September 1795. Samuel FORD [son of Edmond D. Ford] and Ann Crafford Weaver, dau. of John Weaver who consents and is surety. Married 19 Sept.

20 April 1802. Samuel FORD and Martha Haskins, dau. of Benjamin Haskins, deceased. Sur. John T. Ligon. Married 25 April.

20 September 1774. William FORD and Anne Ward, dau. of Joseph Ward.

18 August 1788. Peter FORE, Jr. and Mary Woodson, widow of Charles Woodson. Sur. Jacob Woodson.

19 February 1807. Reuben FORE and Sally Hurt, dau. of John Hurt who is surety.

12 December 1801. John FORREST and Frances Robertson, dau. of William Robertson, deceased. Sur. John Rudd. Married 15 December.

22 November 1783. Ezekiel FOSTER and Alley Murray, dau. of Daniel Murray who is surety. Ezekiel son of Robert Foster who consents. Married 24 November.

Between 1785 and 1787. George W. FOSTER and Julia Flournoy. Marriage register says June 1785.

January 1794. George FOSTER and   Price. Order Book. January Court.

9 February 1795. George FOSTER and Elizabeth Ann Hamblen, dau. of John Hamblen, deceased. Sur. William Hamblen. Married 12 February.

31 May 1797. George FOSTER and Agnes Mitchell, dau. of John and Elizabeth Mitchell who consent. Sur. James Davis Hill. Married 6 June. Marriage register says 6 June 1796.

17 December 1802. George FOSTER and Jane May, dau. of John May, deceased. Sur. William Loving. Married 19 Dec.

18 September 1807. James J. FOSTER and Mary Gibson, dau. of Thomas Gibson, deceased. Sur. Robert B. Gibson. Marriage register says Married 2 December.

9 March 1784. John FOSTER and Elizabeth Wilks. Marriage Register.

5 February 1791. Larkin FOSTER and Polly Cawthorn. Sur. Thomas Cawthorn. Married 27 February.

28 August 1805. Jennings FOWLKES and Elizabeth Carter, dau. of Waddell Carter, deceased. Sur. Larkin Anderson.

26 December 1787. Ludwell FOSTER and Sally Holt, dau. of Plunkett Holt who consents. Sur. James Nott. Ludwell son of Thomas Foster. Married 27 December.

11 January 1788. Robert FOSTER and Tabitha Jackson, dau. of Thomas Jackson who consents. Sur. William Foster. Married 14 February.

12 February 1795. Robert FOSTER and Elizabeth Hankins. Minister's returns.

25 August 1761. Thomas FOSTER and Caroline Rogers. Sur. Peter LeGrand. Thomas Foster of Cumberland Co.

20 November 1799. William FOSTER and Molly Crockett, dau. of John Crockett. Sur. William Mitchell. Married 23 November.

31 December 1807. William FOSTER and Susanna Sharpe, dau. of Josiah Sharpe who is surety.

18 September 1797. Austin FOWLKES and Polly Prince Pulliam, dau. of George Pulliam, deceased. Sur. John Woodfin. Married 21 September. Marriage Register says Polly Price.

23 November 1802. Bass FOWLKES and Polly R. Wootten, dau. of William Wootten who consents. Sur. Jesse Wootten.

27 December 1798. Daniel FOWLKES and Sarah Hines, dau. of William Hines. Sur. Archer Fowlkes. Daniel son of Daniel Fowlkes Sr. who consents.

18 May 1795. Hezekiah FOWLKES and Sally Smith, dau. of Henry Smith, deceased. Sur. John Fowlkes.

1 August 1801. Joel FOWLKES and Betsy Pulliam, dau. of George Pulliam, deceased. Sur. John Woodfin. Married 5 August.

21 July 1788. John FOWLKES and Judith Penick, dau. of Mary Penick who consents. Sur. Thomas Penick. Another record says dau. of John and Mary (Mallory) Penick.

16 December 1799. Nathan FOWLKES and Betty Wootten, dau. of William Wootten who consents. Sur. Nathan Penick.

21 December 1809. Nathan FOWLKES and Lucy Armes, dau. of James Armes who is surety.

20 February 1804. Thompson FOWLKES and Elizabeth Philips, dau. of Richard Philips who consents. Sur. Laban Neal. Married 24 February.

17 August 1789. William FOWLKES and Polly Clarke, dau. of John Clarke. Sur. John Clarke, Jr.

8 April 1802. William FOWLKES and Patsy Anderson, dau. of Worsham Anderson who is surety.

2 October 1794. Robert FRANKLIN and Mary Shackleton, widow of William Shakleton. Sur. Moses Tredway.

17 October 1792. William FRANKLIN and Milley Jackson, dau. of Thomas Jackson, deceased. Sur. Robert Foster.

21 May 1800. George FRIEND and Nancy Ligon, dau. of James Ligon who consents. Sur. Owen Haskins.

12 January 1801. Archibald FUQUA and Sally Clarke, dau. of Thomas Clarke who consents. Sur. Joseph Ligon. Married 13 January.

6 April 1785. Obadiah FUQUA and Mary Morton, dau. of John Morton. Sur. Francis Watkins.

19 December 1805. Peyton FUQUA and Mary McGehee, dau. of Jacob McGehee who consents. Sur. David Holt, Jr. Married 26 December.

14 December 1789. William FUQUA and Sally Morton, dau. of John Morton. Sur. Josiah Morton.

24 December 1808. William FUQUA and Martha Chappell, widow of Samuel Chappell. Sur. Richard Phillips. Married 27 Dec.

17 December 1787. Francis GAINES and Nancy Baker, dau. of Caleb Baker who is surety.

3 November 1791. Peter GALLAHORN and Sarah Davis. Minister's returns. See Peter Gollahorn.

10 June 1760. John GANNAWAY and Mary Byrum (widow). Sur. Abraham Venable, Jr. (John Gannaway the Elder.)

19 September 1760. James GARDEN and Sarah Wimbish. Sur. James Wimbish.

17 November 1808. John GARNETT and Sally Gray, dau. of William Gray who is surety.

4 July 1794. Thomas GARRETT and Frances Wade, dau. of Philip Wade who consents. Sur. Hampton Wade.

14 November 1801. Alexander GAULDING, Jr. and Betsy Cason, dau. of Seth Cason, deceased. Sur. Richard Gaulding.

4 January 1793. Freeman GAULDING and Judith Holloway, dau. of John Holloway who consents. Sur. Thomas Jones. Married 8 January.

6 December 1794. John GAULDING and Sally Cawthorn, dau. of Richard Cawthorn, deceased and Catherine Cawthorn. Sur. Philemon G. Cawthorn. Married 18 December.

14 April 1808. John GAULDING and Martha Gaulding, dau. of Jesse Gaulding who is surety.

23 December 1788. Joseph GAULDING and Patty Barnett, dau. of Richard Barnett, deceased and Mary Barnett. Sur. Alexander Gaulding. Married 24 December.

17 December 1798. Charles D. GEORGE and Elizabeth Rowlett, dau. of Mackness Rowlett who consents. Sur. Stephen Neal. Married 19 December.

16 May 1785. Thomas GIBBERTON and Leah Standefer, dau. of Fanny Standefer. Sur. Ezekiel Hendrick. Thomas over 22.

2 November 1793. Mathew GIBBS and Sally Rowlett, dau. of John and Edith Rowlett who consent. Sur. John Penick.

14 August 1809. Samuel GILCHRIST and Polly J. Davis, dau. of Nicholas Davis, deceased. Sur. Anderson Lumpkin.

7 September 1791. John GILLELAND and Polly Martin, dau. of Margaret Martin. Sur. Henry Young. Married 19 September.

26 September 1792. William GILLELAND and Nancy Johnson, dau. of Philip Johnson who is surety. Married 27 Sept.

5 January 1764. James GILLESPIE and Elizabeth Finley, dau. of John Finley, Sr. who consents. Sur. Robert Baker. James Gillespie of Augusta County.

12 June 1783. William GILLESPIE and Agnes Ritchie. Minister's returns.

21 May 1792. William GILLESPIE and Sarah Jones, dau. of Thomas Jones, deceased. Sur. Augustus Watson. Married 26 May.

6 October 1798. James GILLIAM and Patsey Mathews, dau. of Philip Mathews who consents. Sur. James Hill. Married 10 October.

3 October 1805. John H. GILLIAM and Lucy Bennett, dau. of William Bennett who consents. Sur. Southy Bell.

16 December 1799. William GILLIAM and Judith Woodson, dau. of Charles Woodson, deceased. Her guardian Robert Kelso consents. Sur. Jacob Woodson.

13 February 1799. Willis GLASS and Nancy Dupuy, dau. of Stephen Dupuy who is surety. Willis Glass of Halifax Co.; son of John Glass who consents.

11 December 1784. Daniel GLENN and Anne Venable, dau. of Charles Venable who consents. Sur. Robert Venable. Married 20 December.

20 December 1790. Gideon GLENN and Sally Lancaster. Sur. Nathaniel Lancaster.

3 October 1809. Peyton GLENN and Ann Calhoon, dau. of Adam Calhoon, deceased. Sur. Adam Calhoon. Marriage register says Ann Colquhorn.

18 January 1804. Daniel GODSEY and Patsey Shepherd, dau. of Isaac Shepherd who consents. Sur. Marshall Seay. Married 19 January.

23 June 1792. David GOLLAHER and Mary Ann Trower, dau. of John Trower who consents. Sur. Thomas Gibbons. Married 30 June. See David Gollerhorn.

29 October 1805. William GOLLAHON and Sally Kitchen, dau. of Toley and Elizabeth Kitchen who consent. Sur. William Gilliland.

30 June 1792. David GOLLERHORN and Maryan Trowers. Minister's returns. See David Gollaher.

17 October 1791. Peter GOLLAHORN and Sarah Davis, dau. of William Davis. Sur. William Morgan. Married 3 November. See Peter Gallahorn.

5 July 1790. John C. GOODE and Dolly Venable, dau. of Charles Venable who consents. Sur. Peyton Glenn.

19 February 1794. John GOODE and Sarah Montagert, dau. of Philip Montagert. Sur. Philip McTagert. Married 20 February. Minister's returns say Sarah M. Taggart.

24 January 1765. Robert GOODE and Sarah Collier. Son of Samuel Goode who consents. James Scott consents for Sarah. Sur. Mackerness Goode. Both parties of Chesterfield Co.

12 December 1796. William GOODE and Agnes Holloway, widow of Nathaniel Holloway, and dau. of Charles Venable who consents and is surety. Married 24 December. Agnes Venable married Nathaniel Holloway 13 February 1794.

20 October 1789. Thomas GORDON and Susanna Kelley, dau. of John Kelley. Sur. Patrick Kelley.

2 October 1787. John GRAY and Lucy Jones, dau. of Henry Jones who is surety. Married 4 October.

28 March 1800. William GRAY and Judy Tyree, dau. of William Tyree who consents. Sur. George King.

21 December 1784. Parrish GREEN and Patty Wade. Sur. Francis Watkins. Parrish son of Thomas Green who consents. Married 23 December.

21 November 1785. Thomas GREEN, Jr. and Elizabeth Julia Booker, dau. of William Booker, deceased. Consent of Mother, Mary Booker. Sur. Walthall Halcombe.

15 November 1791. John GREENWOOD and Susanna Baker, dau. of Caleb Baker who consents. Sur. Thomas Jeffress. John son of Thomas Greenwood who consents. Married 16 November.

26 July 1797. Robert GREENWOOD and Patsy Baker, dau. of Caleb Baker who is surety.

24 December 1779. Thomas GREGORY and Molly Lancaster, dau. of Nathaniel Lancaster who consents. Sur. Michael Maddox.

23 November 1799. Thomas GRIMES and Rebecca Hamilton, dau. of Alexander Hamilton, deceased. Mother, Elizabeth Hamilton, consents. Sur. Alexander Hamilton. Married 26 Nov.

15 December 1788. Alexander GUILL, Jr. and Betty Hubbard, dau. of John Hubbard who consents. Sur. John Fielder.

11 March 1800. Josiah GUILL and Peggy Hughes, dau. of John Hughes. Sur. Nathaniel Guill.

19 December 1801. Reuben GUILL and Mildred Shepard, dau. of Robert Shepard. Sur. Samuel Shepard. Married 24 Dec.

18 July 1796. Russell GUILL and Elizabeth Cawthorn, dau. of Thomas Cawthorn who is surety. Russell son of Alexander Guill.

15 January 1789. William GUILL and Betsy Brightwell, dau. of Reynolds Brightwell who consents. Sur. Charles Brightwell.

20 February 1786. John GUNTER and Elizabeth Hill, dau. of John Hill who is surety. Married 24 February.

1 November 1792. Robert HADEN and Mary H. Miller, dau. of John Miller who consents. Sur. William Miller. Married 3 November. See Robert Hudson.

30 August 1803. Richard HADEN and Lucy Goode, dau. of Robert Goode. Sur. Hendley Haden. Anthony Haden, father of Richard Haden consents.

18 April 1797. Matthew HAIRFIELD and Patsy Fielder, dau. of Thomas Fielder, deceased, and Ann Fielder who consents. Sur. John Fielder.

15 April 1793. Samuel HALL and Mary Selby, dau. of Charles Selby who is surety. Married 25 April. Minister's returns say Sally Selby.

19 October 1795. Stephen HALL and Nancy Dejarnett, dau. of John T. Dejarnett, deceased. Sur. John Purnall. Married 21 October.

15 September 1800. Thomas HALL and Anne Simmons, dau. of Thomas Simmons who is surety.

20 October 1800. Daniel HAMBLEN and Elizabeth Thompson, dau. of Robert Thompson, deceased. Consent of her guardian John Wingo. Sur. Elijah Hudson. Married 23 October.

28 February 1797. William HAMBLEN and Sally Geers, dau. of Thomas Geers who is surety.

12 May 1766. John HAMILTON and Christian Richie. Sur. Charles Richie.

4 November 1803. John HAMILTON and Margaret P. Downes, dau. of William Downes, deceased. Sur. Robert Hill.

23 November 1807. Bedford HAMLETT and Mary G. Wootton, dau. of Jesse Wootton who consents. Sur. Samuel Morgan. James Hamlett, father of Bedford, consents.

20 May 1806. George HAMLETT and Nancy O. Wootten, dau. of William Wootten who consents. Sur. Samuel Wootten. Married 22 May.

24 September 1796. Jesse HAMLETT and Elizabeth Clarke, dau. of John Clarke, deceased. Consent of her guardian Susanna Clarke. Sur. Richard Royall. Married 13 October.

16 January 1809. James HANNAH and Elizabeth Nimmo, dau. of William Nimmo, deceased. Sur. James Nimmo. Married 18 Jan.

8 December 1761. Robert HANNA, Jr. and Mary Cunningham, dau. of Mathew Cunningham who consents. Sur. Robert Hanna, Sr.

18 September 1781. George HANNAH and Maryan Patterson. Marriage Register.

4 April 1799. John HARDYMAN and Susannah Baldwin, dau. of John Baldwin who is surety.

20 December 1792. Joseph HARGRAVE and Caty Gray, dau. of Charles Gray who consents. Sur. Archey Gray. Married 22 December. 1793? See Joseph Hargrove.

31 August 1797. Thomas HARGRAVE and Elizabeth McDearmon, dau. of Bryan McDearmon who consents. Sur. James McDearmon. See Thomas Hartgrove.

22 December 1793. Joseph HARGROVE and Caty Gray. Minister's returns. See Joseph Hargrave.

26 December 1805. Asa HARPER and Frances Rice, dau. of Samuel Rice who is surety. Married 28 December.

14 December 1802. John HARPER and Frances Rowlett, dau. of Mackness Rowlett who is surety.

23 October 1805. Samuel HARPER and Rebecca Williamson, dau. of Robert Williamson, deceased. Sur. Robert Williamson.

20 April 1803. Benjamin HARRIS and Sally Ellyson, dau. of John Ellyson. Sur. Charles Woodson. Married 1802.

27 December 1791. Edward HARRIS and Rhoda Arnold, dau. of John Arnold who consents. Sur. Terry Arnold. Married 29 December.

16 December 1805. Gideon HARRIS and Martha Gilliam, dau. of James Gilliam who consents. Sur. John H. Gilliam. Married 24 December.

20 November 1787. Graves HARRIS and Elizabeth Baldwin, dau. of John Baldwin who is surety.

8 July 1783. Micajah HARRIS and Patsy Davison, dau. of Mary Davison who consents. Sur. John Chambers.

10 July 1782. Micajah HARRIS and Polly Davison. Both marriages given.

16 December 1790. Ralph HARRIS and Agnes Baldwin, Sur. John Baldwin.

11 April 1809. William C. HARRIS and Anna H. Dabney, dau. of John Dabney, Sr. who consents. Sur. John Dabney, Jr. Married 18 April.

19 May 1809. Christopher HARRISON and Nancy Binns, dau. of Wiltshire Binns who consents. Sur. John H. Craddock.

8 January 1784. John HARRISON and Mary Magdalen Robertson, Consent of Isaac Robertson. Sur. James Loaker. Married 9 January.

8 January 1784. John HARRISON and Magdalene Robertson, dau. of Jesse Robertson. Sur. James Loaker. Evidently the same couple.

13 August 1804. William HARRISON and Sophia Smith, dau. of Owen Smith who consents. Sur. Robert Hawkins.

14 September 1797. Thomas HARTGROVE and Elizabeth Mackdearman. Minister's returns. See Thomas Hargrave.

12 September 1808. John HARVEY and Anna Tyree, dau. of William Tyree, Sr., who consents. Sur. Flanders Tyree.

17 November 1788. Edward HASKINS and Lucy Carter, dau. of Waddle Carter, deceased. Sur. Samuel Carter.

3 June 1797. Edward HASKINS and Elizabeth Walthall, dau. of Christopher Walthall. Sur. Joseph Ligon. Married 8 June.

4 October 1791. John N. HASKINS and Nancy Walthall, dau. of Christopher Walthall who consents. Sur. John Walthall. Married 8 October.

26 April 1756. Thomas HASKINS and Ann Nash. Sur. John Nash, Jr.

25 October 1803. John HATCHETT and Sally A. Redd, dau. of Thomas Redd, deceased, and Frances Redd. Sur. Thomas Jones, Jr.

20 February 1802. William HATTEN and Tabitha Young, dau. of Thomas Young, deceased. Sur. Joseph Jordan. Married 27 Feb.

18 July 1791. Benjamin HAWKINS and Nancy Perkinson, dau. of John Perkinson who consents. Sur. Laban Hawkins. Married 10 August.

20 August 1810. Benjamin HAWKINS and Elizabeth Fowlkes, widow of Thompson Fowlkes, dau. of Richard Philips. Sur. John Booth.

16 September 1803. Brackett HAWKINS and Polly Geers, dau. of Thomas Geers who consents. Sur. Dread Holeman. Married 1 October. Minister's returns say Polly Gears.

6 February 1810. Joel HAWKINS and Susanna Deshazer, dau. of John Deshazer, deceased. Sur. John W. Ellington. Laban Hawkins consents for son Joel. Married 8 February.

7 April 1797. Obadiah HAWKINS and Sally Hudgins, dau. of William Hudgins. Sur. Laban Hawkins.

17 December 1787. Robert HAWKINS and Elizabeth Smith. Sur. Owen Smith.

20 September 1808. Robert HAWKINS and Sally Gilliam, dau. of James Gilliam who consents. Sur. William Matthews.

20 September 1786. Lewis HAWKS and Patsy Blanton, dau. of Joshua Blanton who is surety. Married 22 September. Minister's returns say Betty Blanton.

16 December 1782. Richard HAYS and Mary Ann Smith, dau. of George Smith who is surety. Richard Hays of Lunenburg Co.

18 March 1801. Elijah HENDRICK and Kitty G. Baker, dau. of Caleb Baker who is surety.

23 December 1781. Ezekiel HENDRICK and Mary Wood, her own consent. Sur. John Fielder.

. John HIGGINSON and Frances Hudson, dau. of William Hudson who is surety.

20 March 1783. Patrick HIGONS and Mary Wood.

6 October 1798. James HILL and Lucy Mathews, dau. of Philip Mathews. Sur. James Gilliam. Married 10 October.

20 January 1796. John HILL and Elizabeth Thompson, dau. of Thomas Thompson who is surety. Married 4 February.

28 January 1803. John HILL and Nancy Arnold, dau. of John Arnold who is surety. Married 1 February.

18 January 1796. Robert HILL and Elizabeth Franklin, dau. of Benjamin Franklin who is surety. Married 28 January.

2 December 1807. Thomas HILL and Betsy Mathews, dau. of Philip Mathews who consents. Sur. William Mathews. Married 9 December.

2 November 1776. William HILL and Anne Davis. Sur. Davis Hill.

7 January 1765. James HINES and Marrimiar Dejarnett, dau. of Elias and Elizabeth Dejarnett who consent. Sur. John Thomas Dejarnett. See Joseph Hines.

28 January 1803. John HINES and Frances North, dau. of John North, deceased. Sur. Thomas Hines.

7 January 1765. Joseph HINES and Marrimiar Dejarnett, dau. of Elias and Elizabeth Dejarnett who consent. Sur. John Thomas Dejarnett. See James Hines.

4 January 1806. Joseph HINES and Judith Spaulding, dau. of John Spaulding. Sur. Thomas Hines.

18 December 1809. Thomas HINES and Nancy Hines, dau. of Henry Hines who is surety.

12 December 1809. William HINES and Sally Fears, dau. of James Fears, deceased. Sur. William Carter. Married 21 Dec.

14 June 1807. Clarence HINGE and Mary Woldridge. Minister's returns.

3 February 1797. Archibald HIX and Nancy Woodson, dau. of Jacob Woodson who is surety. Married 16 February.

16 February 1797. Archibald HIX and Mary Woodson. Minister's returns. Evidently same as above.

24 August 1772. John HOLCOMBE and Martha Venable, dau. of Abraham Venable. Sur. Francis Watkins.

21 October 1806. Ethelread (Dread) HOLEMAN and Nancy Geers, dau. of Thomas Geers. Sur. John Penick. Married 11 Nov.

16 February 1793. James HOLEMAN and Frankie Spencer, dau. of Sharpe Spencer who is surety. Married 21 February.

9 February 1796. Gregory HOLLOWAY and Hannah Allen, dau. of James Allen, who is surety. Married 11 February.

1 February 1794. Nathaniel HOLLOWAY and Agnes Venable, dau. of Charles Venable who consents. Sur. Charles Venable, Jr. Married 13 February.

15 November 1796. Daniel HOLT and Betsy Young, dau. of Stephen Young who consents. Sur. William Rutledge.

29 October 1802. David HOLT and Elizabeth McGehee, dau. of Jacob McGehee who consents. Sur. Thomas Clarke.

12 February 1778. Jesse HOLT and Mary Ward, dau. of Joseph Ward of Henrico Co. Sur. Samuel Goode. Jesse Holt of Amelia Co.

20 January 1800. John HOLT and Henrietta Smith, dau. of Henry and Mary Smith. Sur. Henry Ligon.

19 October 1786. Josiah HOLT and Sarah Jackson, dau. of Thomas Jackson who consents. Sur. James Holt. Josiah son of Plunkett Holt who consents.

30 September 1806. Richard HOLT and Nancy Deshazer, dau. of Henry Deshazer who consents. Sur. David Holt. Married 6 October.

1 October 1804. William HOLT and Jemima Rowlett, dau. of John Rowlett who is surety. Married 11 October.

19 November 1810. William HOLT and Judith Penick, dau. of John Penick who is surety.

11 September 1794. William HOOD and Sarah Fears, dau. of Absalom Fears who consents. Sur. Archilaus Fears.

17 October 1808. John HOWELL and Jenny Dickenson, dau. of Nelson Dickerson, deceased. Sur. James Dickerson. Minister's returns say Jenny Dixon.

15 April 1792. Richard HOWELL and Frances Ayers. Sur. George Walton.

12 December 1786. Benjamin HUBBARD and Patty Richards, dau. of John Richards who is surety. Married 18 December. Minister's return says Polly Richards.

4 September 1782. Charles HUDSON and Martha Biggars, widow. Sur. Nathaniel Allen.

3 September 1791. Elijah HUDSON and Mary Thompson, dau. of Robert Thompson. Sur. Samuel Morton.

14 January 1772. John HUDSON and Elizabeth Mason, dau. of Joseph Mason who is surety.

3 June 1790. John HUDSON and Lucy Baker, dau. of Caleb Baker. Sur. John Clark. Married 5 June.

8 January 1801. John HUDSON and Prudence Rutledge, dau. of Thomas Rutledge who consents. Sur. William Rutledge.

12 November 1808. John HUDSON and Judith Rutledge. Minister's returns. See Joshua Hudson.

12 November 1808. Joshua HUDSON and Judith Rutledge, dau. of Thomas Rutledge, deceased. Sur. Thomas Rutledge. See John Hudson.

20 February 1797. Richard HUDSON and Susannah Parrott, dau. of Nathaniel Parrott, deceased. Sur. James Hudson.

3 November 1792. Robert HUDSON and Mary H. Miller. Minister's returns. See Robert Haden.

21 July 1775. William HUDSON and Mary Watkins, dau. of John Watkins, deceased. Sur. John Watkins.

19 October 1807. Jesse HUGHES and Mary Woodson Cheadle, dau. of John Cheadle who consents. Sur. Thomas F. Cheadle. Married 22 October. Minister's returns say Polly Cheadle.

12 January 1803. Simon HUGHES and Betsy Coleman Bigger, dau. of James Bigger who consents. Sur. Jeremiah Whitworth.

12 January 1803. Simon HUGHES and Betsy Coleman. Evidently the same as above.

21 November 1804. John P. HUNDLEY and Temperance H. Watkins, dau. of Robert Watkins, deceased. Sur. Henry Edward Watkins.

9 February 1784. James HUNT and Christian Mitchell, dau. of John Mitchell. Sur. James Mitchell. James Hunt of Charlotte Co.

18 July 1785. Francis HURT and Peggy McTaggart, dau. of Philip McTaggart who is surety. Married 27 July. Minister's returns say Peggy Tuggle.

19 December 1785. John HURT and Nelly McTaggart. Sur. Henry Young. Married 27 September 1785. Minister's returns say Nelly Taggart.

15 March 1796. John HURT and Sally Franklin, dau. of Benjamin Franklin who is surety. Married 29 March.

2 January 1796. Josias (Jonas?) HURT and Elizabeth Young, dau. of Henry Young, deceased. Guardian, Obediah Jenkins consents. Sur. Thomas E. Young. Married 7 January. Obadiah Jenkins was her brother-in-law, husband of her older sister, Sarah Young.

7 January 1796. Josiah HURT and Elizabeth Young. Minister's returns.

27 October 1804. Meriwether HURT and Mary Ann Redd, dau. of John Redd who is surety.

19 May 1783. Obadiah HURT and Winnie Beasley. Sur. Ezekiel Hendrick.

12 February 1802. Obadiah HURT and Nancy Davenport. Minister's returns.

7 June 1787. Zachariah HURT and Fanny Mitchell, dau. of John Mitchell who is surety. Married 8 June.

14 November 1782. John HUTCHERSON and Elizabeth Cannon. Minister's returns.

2 December 1796. John HUSTON and Elizabeth Whitworth, dau. of William Whitworth who consents. Sur. Jeremiah Whitworth. Married 3 December.

13 July 1775. William HUTSON and Mary Watkins, dau. of Thomas Watkins who consents.

13 June 1807. Claiborne INGE and Mary Wooldridge, dau. of Simon Wooldridge who consents. Sur. James Franklin. See Clarence Inge.

14 June 1807. Clarence INGE and Mary Wooldridge. Marriage Register. See Claiborne Inge.

27 April 1793. Abel JACKSON and Patsy Jackson, dau. of Matthew Jackson who consents. Sur. William Jackson.

25 October 1804. Curtis JACKSON and Elizabeth Oliver, dau. of John Oliver, deceased. Sur. John Oliver.

12 June 1809. Curtis JACKSON and Sally Webber, dau. of Simon Webber. Sur. Francis Jackson. Married 14 June.

4 January 1806. Edwin JACKSON and Jane Penick, dau. of Thomas Penick who is surety. Married 15 January. See Edward Jackson.

15 January 1806. Edward JACKSON and Jane Penick, dau. of Thomas and Kesiah (Owen) Penick. See Edwin Jackson.

2 February 1789. Francis JACKSON and Elizabeth Childers, dau. of John Childers who consents. Sur. Robert Foster.

10 November 1761. Hezekiah JACKSON and Elizabeth Pamplet. Sur. George Walton.

11 May 1807. Hezekiah JACKSON and Judith Gaulding, dau. of Alexander Gaulding who is surety. Married 14 May.

22 March 1785. John JACKSON and Nancy Going (Gowing). Sur. Benjamin Bartlett.

February 1785. John JACKSON and Nancy Jackson.

15 February 1802. Nathaniel JACKSON and Nancy Pankey, dau. of Stephen Pankey, deceased. Sur. Elisha Betts. Married 18 February.

13 September 1785. Philip Whitehead JACKSON and Elizabeth B. Marrable, dau. of Matthew Marrable, deceased. Mother, Mary Marrable consents. Sur. Robert Lawson.

25 January 1808. Stewart JACKSON and Elizabeth W. Coffee, dau. of Thomas Coffee who consents. Sur. Edward Morris. Married 19 May 1807.

10 July 1809. Thomas JACKSON and Martha Deshazer, dau. of John Deshazer, deceased. Sur. Zachariah Rice. Married 12 July. See Thompson Jackson.

12 July 1809. Thompson JACKSON and Martha Deshazer. Minister's returns. See Thomas Jackson.

1 January 1782. William JACKSON and Mary Davidson. Sur. Joshua Davidson. Married 17 January. Minister's returns say Mary Davison.

30 July 1792. William JACKSON and Lydia Oliver, widow of John Oliver, deceased. Sur. Christopher Dejarnett. Married 9 August. William Jackson of Nottoway Co.

21 May 1804. William JACKSON and Polly Hill, dau. of William Hill who is surety.

14 April 1810. William JACKSON and Nancy Thompson, dau. of Arnold Thompson, deceased, and Jane Thompson who consents. Sur. George Davidson.

4 April 1795. Littleberry JENKINS and Mildred Young, dau. of Henry Young, deceased. Sur. Thomas E. Young. Married 9 April.

28 January 1791. Obadiah JENKINS and Sarah Young, dau. of Henry Young, deceased. Sur. Daniel Rather. Married 2 February. Consent of her guardian Robert Venable.

23 January 1797. Clem JENNINGS and Ann W. Cook, dau. of John Cook, Sr. who consents. Sur. John Cook, Jr. Married 26 January.

19 May 1794. David JENNINGS and Sarah Glenn Dabney, dau. of Anna Dabney who consents. Sur. Anderson Dabney. Married 27 May by Rev. William Mahon.

15 November 1798. Richard JENNINGS and Elizabeth Whood, dau. of John Whood, deceased (Wood? K.K.). Sur. Davis Mitchell. Married 17 November.

7 March 1796. Samuel JENNINGS and Judiah Simmons, dau. of John Simmons who consents. Sur. Jehu Simmons.

18 November 1805. William JENNINGS and Polly Smith, dau. of Frightwell Smith, deceased. Sur. Martin Taggart.

13 September 1805. Daniel JOHNS and Polly T. Marshall, dau. of Benejah Marshall who is surety. Married 14 Sept.

19 November 1792. John JOHNSON and Martha Meadows, dau. of Joel Meadows, deceased. Sur. James Bowers. Married 22 November. See John Johnston.

15 October 1792. Philip JOHNSON and Martha Bassett, dau. of Nathaniel Bassett who consents. Sur. Reuben Johnson. Married 18 October. See Philip Johnston.

6 April 1791. Reuben JOHNSON and Charlotte Young, dau. of Carson Young who consents. Sur. James Vaughan.

7 February 1797. Andrew JOHNSTON and Ann Nash, dau. of John Nash. Sur. Abner Nash. Married 9 February.

22 November 1792. John JOHNSTON and Martha Meadows. Minister's returns. See John Johnson.

18 October 1792. Philip JOHNSTON and Martha Bassett. Minister's returns. See Philip Johnson.

25 March 1788. William JOHNSTON and Susanna Bryan, dau. of John Bryan who is surety.

25 February 1809. Anthony D. JONES and Patsy M. Woodson, dau. of Daniel Woodson, deceased and Elizabeth Woodson who consents. Sur. Thomas Linthicum.

27 December 1794. Arthur JONES and Sally Baker, dau. of Caleb Baker who is surety. Married 8 January 1795.

8 November 1770. Henry JONES and Mary Hamlett, dau. of Thomas Hamlett who is surety.

4 April 1805. Henry JONES and Dolly North, dau. of John North, deceased. Guardian Ben Thackston consents. Sur. Elijah Frazier.

8 April 1808. Jacob JONES and Frances Cobb, dau. of Rice Cobb, deceased. Sur. Anthony W. Woodson. Married 16 April.

25 June 1810. Joel JONES and Agnes Gibson, dau. of Thomas Gibson, deceased, and Martha Gibson who consents. Sur. James T. Foster. Guardian, R. Bell, consents. (Whose?) Minister's returns say Joel W. Jones.

16 December 1776. John JONES, Jr. and Elizabeth Eillbank (?) Sur. William Cowan.

25 November 1800. Llewelling JONES and Dorothy Thornton, dau. of Sterling Thornton who is surety.

4 May 1803. Theodrick JONES and Ann Mathews, dau. of William Mathews, deceased. Sur. William T. Mathews. Married 5 May.

20 December 1802. Thomas JONES and Martha Redd, dau. of Thomas Redd, deceased, and Frances Redd who consents. Sur. George Redd. Married 23 December.

24 May 1756. William JONES, Jr. and Jane Bowman, dau. of Brown Bowman who consents. Sur. William Davidson. Consent of William Jones, Sr. father of William, Jr.

30 November 1795. Francis JORDAN and Polly Hudson, dau. of Thomas Hudson who is surety. Married 8 December.

18 April 1791. Matthew JORDAN and Clara Bennett. Sur. William Bennett. Married 5 May. Matthew Jordan son of Matthew Jordan, Sr. who consents.

28 January 1803. Joseph JORDAN and Elizabeth Hatton, dau. of Thomas Hatton who consents. Sur. William Hatton. Married 3 February.

21 May 1793. William JOURNEY and Magdalen Jackson. Minister's returns. See William Jurney.

May 1806. William JOURNEY and Polly North. Minister's returns. See William Jurney.

19 May 1758. Alexander JOYCE and Jane Hamilton. Sur. Alexander Hamilton.

13 October 1781. Benjamin JUDE and Nancy Price, dau. of William Price. Sur. Joseph Price.

20 May 1793. William JURNEY and Magdalene Jackson, dau. of Rowland Jackson, deceased. Sur. John Dupuy. Married 21 May. See William Journey.

24 May 1806. William JURNEY and Polly North, dau. of John North, deceased. Sur. James Dodson. See William Journey.

30 September 1793. Daniel KELLY and Mary Brooks, dau. of Thomas Brooks, deceased. Consent of Mary Brooks. Sur. William Weakley. Married 2 October.

23 April 1800. John KELLY and Tillithicum Swinney, dau. of William Swinney who consents and is surety. Married 24 Apr.

2 June 1795. Edward KERZEY and Susannah Leneve. Sur. John Leneve.

17 December 1799. John KEY and Elizabeth Watson, dau. of Samuel Watson Sr. Sur. Samuel Watson.

10 February 1792. James KIDD and Edith Murray, dau. of Daniel Murray, deceased. Sur. Thomas Murray.

28 October 1796. George KING and Martha Smithson, dau. of Charles Smithson. Sur. Henry Coleman. Married 29 October.

20 May 1805. Walton KNIGHT and Nancy Hughes Yarbrough, dau. of Joseph Yarbrough who consents. Consent of Woodson Knight father of Walton. Sur. William Morton.

18 June 1781. Woodson KNIGHT and Patty Walton. Marriage Register.

15 December 1800. Noble LADD and Nancy Smith, dau. of George Smith. Sur. Richard Venable.

2 December 1800. Griffin LAMKIN and Betsy Clarke, dau. of James Clarke who consents. Sur. Thomas Clarke. Married 24 December.

17 November 1788. John LANCASTER and Drucilla Legrand, dau. of Alexander Legrand who consents. Sur. Baker Legrand.

20 August 1804. Thomas LANCASTER and Frances Lancaster. Parent, Nathaniel Lancaster who is surety.

15 August 1797. William LANCASTER and Judy Lancaster, dau. of Nathaniel Lancaster who is surety.

18 December 1788. Charles LANDALE and Edith Burks, dau. of Richard Burks who consents. Sur. Robert Hawkins.

17 December 1792. Abraham LEA and Polly Thompson, dau. of Robert Thompson, deceased. Sur. Elijah Hudson. Abraham Lea of Amelia County.

19 December 1805. Coleman LEDBETTER and Tabitha Moss, dau. of James Moss who is surety.

20 December 1809. William LEE and Lucy Elam, dau. of Joel Elam who consents. Sur. Robert Elam.

17 December 1778. Abraham LeGRAND, Jr. and Judith LeGrand. Sur. Alexander LeGrand.

16 November 1798. Alexander LeGRAND, Jr. and Frances Walker, dau. of William Walker, deceased. Sur. Washington Walker. Married 17 November.

8 February 1781. Josiah LeGRAND and Elizabeth Anderson. Sur. Alexander LeGrand.

9 November 1801. Peter LEGRAND and Susannah F. Nash, dau. of John Nash, deceased. Sur. John Nash. Married 12 November.

1 August 1794. John LEIGH and Elizabeth Johns, dau. of Joel Johns who consents. Sur. Paschal G. Leigh.

8 November 1800. Paschal G. LEIGH and Elizabeth Archer Scott, dau. of James Scott who consents. Sur. David G. Leigh. Married 27 November.

January 1781. Henry LEPNER and Susannah Le Neve. (Register) See Henry Lesner.

15 August 1808. Alexander LESLIE and Sarah Duncan, dau. of James Duncan. Sur. William Tyree, Sr. Married 8 September.

January 1781. Henry LESNER and Susanna Leneve. Minister's returns. See Henry Lepner.

10 April 1805. Jacob LESTER and Martha Hamlett, dau. of James Hamlett. Sur. John Mann.

14 January 1788. Moses LEWEILING and Frances Chumbley, dau. of John Chumbley. Sur. Jesse Lewelling.

17 February 1783. William LEWELLING and Hannah Smith. (Register.)

21 March 1791. Benjamin LEWIS and Frances Palmore. Sur. James Holt.

9 October 1803. Charles Joseph LEWIS and Mildred Anderson, Minister's returns. See Joseph Lewis.

16 October 1786. Edward LEWIS and Elizabeth Fleming, dau. of Beverley Fleming, who is surety.

9 April 1801. Elam LEWIS and Martha Hines, dau. of Henry Hines who is surety. Married 17 April.

21 July 1806. Henry LEWIS and Elizabeth Woodson, dau. of Jacob Woodson who is surety.

24 October 1803. Joseph LEWIS and Mildred Anderson, widow of Robert Anderson. Sur. Joel Jackson, Jr. See Charles Joseph Lewis.

26 January 1796. Robert LEWIS and Elinder Jordan, dau. of Robert Jordan, deceased, and Elizabeth Jordan who consents. Sur. Townsom Wilkerson. Married 28 January.

21 March 1785. Henry LIGON and Patty Wootten. Sur. William Wootten. Married   April.

16 November 1801. Henry LIGON and Elizabeth Smith, dau. of Henry Smith, deceased. Sur. Walthall Marshall.

19 December 1774. James LIGON and Sarah Holcombe, dau. of Philip Holcombe. Sur. John Bibb.

21 September 1778. James LIGON and Mary Haskins. Sur. Thomas Haskins.

11 April 1786. John LIGON and Jane Haskins, dau. of Benjamin Haskins. Sur. Edward Haskins.

19 March 1787. John LIGON and Rodith Marshall, dau. of Alexander Marshall who is surety. John son of William Ligon who consents.

18 December 1790. John H. LIGON and no name (probably Elizabeth Guill, dau. of Alexander Guill.) Sur. Charles Brightwell. Married 23 December.

18 January 1796. Joseph LIGON and Ann Clark, dau. of Thomas Clark who is surety.

15 April 1793. Thomas LIGON and Elizabeth Perkinson, dau. of Caleb Perkinson, deceased. Sur. Rowlett Perkinson.

16 September 1805. Thomas D. LIGON and Martha H. Watkins, dau. of Thomas Watkins. Sur. William L. Venable. Married 18 September. Minister's returns say Martha A Watkins.

26 July 1809. Richard LIGON and Fanny McGehee, dau. of Abraham McGehee who is surety.

14 November 1759. William LIGON, Jr. and Edith Turner, dau. of Mary Turner who consents. Sur. Henry Turner.

23 September 1793. William LIGON and Sarah Leigh, dau. of John Leigh, deceased, and Elizabeth Leigh who consents. Sur. Paschal G. Leigh. Married 28 September.

26 December 1806. Joshua LILLARD and Nancy Forrest, dau. of Abraham Forrest who consents. Sur. William T. Ellington.

17 May 1797. William A. LILLY and Nancy Venable, dau. of Charles Venable who consents and is surety. Married 18 May.

15 December 1796. John LIPSCOMBE and Patsy Russell, dau. of Job Russell who is surety.

19 May 1800. Anderson P. LITTLE and Patsey Perkinson, dau. of John Perkinson who consents. Sur. Rowlett Perkinson. Married 22 May.

3 November 1797. Herman LITTLE and Nancy Cunningham, dau. of Josiah Cunningham who consents. Sur. Larkin Anderson. Married 9 November.

8 June 1784. Anderson LLEWELLING and Lucy Rice. (Register.)

20 September 1786. Freeman LLEWELLING and Mary Howell, dau. of Elizabeth Howell who consents. Sur. Jasper Billow (?)

14 January 1788. Moses LLEWELLING and Frances Chumbley, dau. of John Chumbley. Sur. Jesse Llewelling.

19 January 1801. Edmund LOCKETT and Elizabeth Haskins, widow of Edward Haskins. Sur. Branch Walthall. Married 22 January. Dau. of Christopher Walthall.

12 March 1791. Jacob LOCKETT and Lucy Waddle, dau. of Richard Waddle who consents. Sur. John Hutcherson. Married 17 March. Waddell in Register.

19 February 1801. Osborn LOCKETT and Agnes Scott, dau. of James Scott who consents. Sur. Thomas Walton. Married 20 February.

27 October 1797. Royall LOCKETT and Susannah Clark, widow of John Clark, Jr., deceased. Sur. Jesse Hamlett. Married 28 October.

10 May 1779. Robert LORTON and Tabitha Gannaway. Sur. John Morrow, Jr.

26 December 1778. Samuel LOVE and Sally Carter, dau. of Theodrick Carter, deceased. Sur. Francis Watkins.

15 September 1794. Benjamin LOWDER and Sarah Gibbons, dau. of John Gibbons, deceased. Sur. Thomas Gibbons.

1 October 1808. Anderson LUMPKIN and Lucy Davis, widow of Nicholas Davis. Sur. John Curd.

12 April 1808. Obadiah LUMPKIN and Rhoda Brightwell, dau. of Charles Brightwell who is surety. Married 14 April.

21 March 1809. Noah LUNDAMAN and Frances Cobb, dau. of Rice Cobb, deceased. Sur. John Lundaman.

18 January 1786. Redford McCARGO and Lucy Morton. Sur. Richard Morton. Married 26 January. Marriage register says 26 September 1786.

9 January 1800. Nathaniel McCLURG and Polly Redd, dau. of Thomas Redd who consents. Sur. Anderson Redd.

26 November 1808. Samuel McCORMICK and Rebecca Mitchell, dau. of John Mitchell. Sur. Simmons Peck.

24 January 1804. Drury McDEARMON and Nancy Puckett, dau. of David Puckett who is surety. Married 26 January.

1 February 1804. James McDEARMONROE and Sukey Puckett, dau. of David Puckett who is surety.

15 April 1782. James McDOWELL and Hanna Mills. Marriage Register.

2 March 1790. James McDOWELL and Ann Mathews, dau. of Samuel Mathews. Sur. John James.

16 December 1789. Nelson McDOWELL [OF HALIFAX COUNTY] and Susannah Weakley, dau. of James Weakley who consents. Sur. William Weakley.

15 April 1782. James McDUEL and Hannah Mills. Sur. Philip Mathews.

16 April 1804. Adam C. McELROY and Jean Cunningham, dau. of John M. Cunningham who is surety.

7 August 1756. Archibald McELROY and Ann Aston. Sur. Peter Downy. Consent of Will Aston.

19 February 1777. James McELROY and Violet Calhoon, dau. of Adam Calhoon who is surety.

28 March 1782 - 85. Daniel McFALL and Esther Murrain. (Register.)

20 September 1786. Henry McFALL and Sarah White, dau. of Elias White, "late of Hanover Co." Samuel McFall, guardian of Henry is surety. Henry McFall of Henrico Co.

17 September 1787. Abraham McGEHEE and Judith Penick, dau. of William Penick who is surety. Married 3 October. (Judith dau. of William and Judith (Pate?) Penick.)

24 April 1799. Abraham McGEHEE and Polly Hawkins, dau. of Joseph Hawkins, deceased. Sur. Obadiah Hawkins.

16 October 1809. David B. McGEHEE and Elizabeth Clarke, dau. of Thomas Clarke, deceased. Sur. Booker Foster. Married 19 October.

12 December 1781. Jacob McGEHEE and Anne Weaver. Sur. Moore Weaver.

20 June 1768. Mumford McGEHEE and Sally Moore, dau. of John Moore of Charlotte Co. who is surety.

19 October 1778. Samuel McGEHEE and Olive Muse, dau. of William Muse who is surety.

21 October 1805. James W. McGLASSON and Molly Boaz, dau. of Meshac Boaz. Sur. Thomas W. McGlasson. Married 23 Oct.

20 December 1785. Nevin McKINNEY and Lucy Wade. Minister's returns.

29 December 1788. John McMACHEN and Elizabeth Lightfoot. Minister's returns. See John McMahon.

29 December 1788. John McMAHON and Elizabeth Lightfoot. Sur. John Bibb and Claiborne Watkins. See John McMachen.

9 December 1803. James McNEAL and Mary Ann Dowdy, dau. of Richard Dowdy, deceased. Sur. Thomas W. McGlasson.

16 September 1805. Johnson McNEAL and Martha Franklin, dau. of Benjamin Franklin who is surety.

20 December 1793. Ebenezer McROBERT and Mary Foster, dau. of Richard Foster who is surety.

1 January 1794. Ebenezer McROBERT and Mary Foster. Sur. Wm. Mahon. Evidently same as above.

15 October 1792. Theodrick B. McROBERT and Agnes Morton, dau. of Josiah Morton, deceased, of Charlotte Co. Consent of her guardian Jacob Morton. Sur. Archibald McRobert. Married 18 October.

15 March 1785. John McSWINE and Elizabeth Martin. (Register)

15 March 1785. John McSWINNEY and Elizabeth Martin. Evidently same as above.

2 September 1766. John MACK (?) and Sarah Burnett. Sur. John Barksdell.

14 May 1793. Elijah MADDOX and Betsy Brown, dau. of Caleb Brown, deceased. Sur. Richard Peck.

18 September 1780. Michael MADDOX and Elizabeth Lancaster. Sur. Nathaniel Lancaster.

20 October 1800. John MADISON and Nancy Redd, dau. of John Redd who is surety. Married 30 October.

January 1793. Thomas MALLOY and Sarah Moore, dau. of Joseph Moore, deceased. Sur. Nathaniel W. Dandridge, Jr. Married 22 January.

24 July 1799. Drury MALONE and Nancy North, dau. of William North, deceased. Sur. William North.

9 January 1787. Ebenezer MANN and Sarah Moore, dau. of William Moore who consents. Sur. James Mann. Married 11 Jan.

17 March 1788. Joseph MANN and Anne Moore, dau. of William Moore who consents. Sur. William Walker.

10 June 1784. Arthur MARCUM and Frances Howard. (Register) See Arthur Markham.

9 March 1785. Thomas MARKHAM and Nancy Price. Sur. Edmund Price.

8 May 1781 (4?). Arthur MARKHAM and Frances Stowers. Sur. Charles Scott. See Arthur Marcum.

23 October 1781. Zophar MARSH and Sarah Moore. Sur. Rial Moore.

9 November 1802. Zopher MARSH and Jane Woodrum, dau. of William Woodrum, deceased. Sur. William Childress, Jr. Married 10 November.

2 September 1795. Alexander MARSHALL and Millincer Burks, widow of George Burks. Sur. William Wooten. Married 4 September, 1794. Minister's returns say Milne Burks.

7 March 1796. Richard MARSHALL and Sally Phillips, dau. of Richard Phillips who consents. Sur. Laban Hawkins.

21 December 1807. Francis A. MARTIN and Ann M. Overstreet, dau. of John H. Overstreet who consents. Sur. James Madison. Married 23 December.

29 October 1810. John MARTIN and Thirsa Hill, dau. of William Hill who is surety.

20 March 1769. Robert MARTIN and Mary Venable. Sur. Charles Venable.

21 February 1803. Robert MARTIN and Mary Adams, dau. of Robert Adams, deceased. Sur. Thomas Jackson. Married 22 February.

9 December 1806. Robert MARTIN and Amy Brightwell, dau. of Reynold Brightwell, deceased, and Drucilla Brightwell who consents. Sur. William Gilliland. Amy age 21.

25 September 1789. James MASON and Nancy Williams, dau. of William Williams who is surety.

25 December 1783. John MASON and Mary Mason, dau. of Joseph Mason who consents.

6 February 1792. Jonathan MASON and Elizabeth Berry, dau. of Joshua Berry who is surety. Married 9 February.

14 November 1782. Antonio MASSEY and Lucy Howell. (Register.)

5 March 1788. Charles MASSEY and Elizabeth Davis, dau. of William Davis. Sur. Charles Selbee (?)

20 June 1796. Sherwood MASSEY and Sally Smith, dau. of John Smith who is surety. Sherrard Massey in Register. Married 7 July.

5 February 1794. Nathaniel MATHEWS and Alice Archdeacon, dau. of Ann Archdeacon who consents. Sur. Wm. Russell. Married 6 February.

26 October 1781. Claiborne MATTOX and Jane Morrow. (Register.)

16 August 1785. John MAYS and Elizabeth Lewis, dau. of David Lewis who is surety.

7 February 1789. Benjamin MEADOWS and Polly Morris, dau. of Sylvanus Morris who consents. Sur. Josiah Williams of Amelia Co.

18 September 1809. Isaac MEADOWS and Caroline Baugh, dau. of John Baugh, deceased. Sur. Robert Hill.

29 October 1798. John Anderson MEADOWS and Letty Cunningham, dau. of Josiah Cunningham who is surety.

17 April 1786. Obadiah MEADOWS and Prudence Wells, dau. of Frederick Wells who is surety.

6 May 1791. Joseph METTAUER and Jemima Gaulding. Sur. Richard Watkins.

21 January 1799. James MICKLE and Jane Elam, dau. of John Elam who is surety. Married 7 February.

21 December 1795. William MICKLE and Darkus Little, dau. of Margaret Little who consents. Sur. John Taggart. Married 7 January 1796. (Dorcas).

18 May 1807. John MILES and Anna Chumley, dau. of John Chumley, deceased. Sur. William Keeling. Married 26 May.

22 May 1800. Anderson P. MILLER and Patsy Perkinson. Minister's returns.

15 August 1796. Armstead MILLER and Susannah Redd, dau. of George Redd who is surety.

26 September 1799. John MILLER and Nancy Ellington, dau. of Hezekiah Ellington who is surety. Married 10 October.

8 August 1792. Jeremiah MILLER and Sarah H. Ligon, dau. of James Ligon who consents. Sur. Phil Holcombe, Jr. Married 9 August.

17 December 1804. Richard A. MILLER and Rebecca Ellington, Hezekiah and Ridley Ellington who consent. Sur. John Miller.

20 November 1800. Samuel MILLS and Susanna Foster, dau. of George Pollard Foster who is surety. Married 27 November.

7 January 1795. William MILLS and Mary Wallace, dau. of John Wallace, deceased. Sur. Peter Thomas. Married 11 Jan.

27 June 1810. Nathaniel P. MIMS and Clarissa H. Perkinson, dau. of Josiah Perkinson who consents. Sur. Henry Walthall. Married 28 June.

John MINER and Mary Burke. Sur. Thompson Burke.

31 October 1800. David MITCHELL and Polly Peck, dau. of William Peck who consents. Sur. Jeffrey Peck. Married 26 November. Minister's returns say Polly Peek.

24 October 1808. Henry MITCHELL and Susannah Foster, dau. of Anthony Foster, deceased, and Ann Foster who consents. Sur. William Lavern. Married 25 October.

12 March 1781. James MITCHELL and Conny Cook. Sur. John Mitchell. See Joseph Mitchell.

20 January 1758. John MITCHELL and Martha Gilliam. Sur. Charles Gilliam.

28 February 1782. John MITCHELL and Agnes Matthews. (Register.)

12 March 1781. Joseph MITCHELL and Conny Cook. Sur. John Mitchell. See James Mitchell.

9 November 1779. Robert MITCHELL and Margaret Mann, dau. of Fergus Mann who consents. Sur. John Mann.

19 November 1804. Robert MITCHELL and Agnes Peek, dau. of William Peek, deceased and Esther Peek who consents. Sur. Richard Peek.

10 October 1798. Thomas MITCHELL and Sally Cook, dau. of John Cook, Sr. who is surety. Married 13 October.

8 November 1800. William MITCHELL, Jr. and Sarah Porter, dau. of Andrew and Margaret Porter who consent. Sur. Benjamin Giles. Married 13 November.

20 February 1802. William MITCHELL and Fanny League, dau. of James League who is surety. Married 25 February.

John G. MOORE and Elizabeth Walker, dau. of Thomas Walker, Jr. who consents. Consent only - no date.

6 October 1801. John MOORE and Nancy Booker, dau. of George Booker. Sur. Francis Watkins, Jr. Married 18 Oct.

22 March 1774. Thomas MOORE and Nancy Hughes Walton, dau. of George Walton who consents. Sur. Joseph Moore.

17 November 1802. Thomas MOORE and Polly V. Moore (Moon), dau. of Archibald Moon, deceased. Sur. Theodrick B. McRobert. Married 18 October 1803. Thomas son of Thomas Moore Sr. of Columbia Co. Georgia who consents.

15 August 1810. William W. MOORE and Tabitha Ellett, widow of Archibald Ellett. Sur. James A. Armes. Married 16 August.

19 December 1808. James B. MORGAN, Jr. and Ann Mosby Johnson, dau. of John Johnson. Sur. James B. Morgan Sr.

20 August 1795. John MORGAN and Lena (?) Tucker, dau. of Matthew Tucker, deceased. Sur. William Black. Married 10 September.

21 February 1803. Joseph MORGAN and Polly Young, dau. of Henry Young, deceased. Sur. James Ewing, Jr. Married 3 Mar.

15 October 1796. Terry MORGAN and Jane Hill, dau. of John Hill who is surety.

28 July 1806. Robert MORGAN and Christian Ritchie, dau. of Hugh Ritchie. Sur. Alexander Ritchie. Married 31 July.

14 November 1808. William MORGAN and Lucy Haskins, dau. of Edward Haskins. Sur. Augustus Watson.

17 October 1807. William MORGAN and Polly B. Hudson, dau. of James Hudson, deceased. Sur. Irby Hudson. Guardian Jesse Wootten consents. William Morgan of Nottoway Co.

15 December 1794. Dabney MORRIS and Sally Perkinson, dau. of John Perkinson who is surety.

5 January 1808. John MORRIS and Nancy Holland, dau. of Dick Holland, deceased. Sur. Joel Watkins. Married 7 Jan.

6 February 1776. Nathaniel MORRIS and Nancy Jeffries, dau. of Nathaniel Jeffries "of said county". Sur. Benjamin Morris. Nathaniel Morris of Buckingham Co.

7 August 1808. Osborne MORRIS and Polly Raine, dau. of John Raine, deceased. Guardian James McGehee consents. Sur. John Forrest. Married 12 August. Minister's returns say Polly Rains.

12 September 1781. John MORROW, Jr. and Mary Scott, dau. of Saymore Scott who consents. Sur. Michael Maddox.

1 January 1792. Archibald MORTON and Elizabeth Woodall, dau. of William Woodall who consents. Sur. David Tinsley. Married 5 January.

25 September 1804. Charles MORTON and Polly Lockett, dau. of Stephen Lockett. Sur. Osborne Lockett.

6 September 1774. Jacob MORTON and Jane Davis Booker, dau. of William Booker who is surety.

19 December 1799. John MORTON and Tabitha Penick, dau. of William and Judith Penick. Marriage register.

24 November 1784. Jonathan MORTON and Letty McCargo, dau. of John McCargo who is surety. Married 25 November.

15 October 1796. Joseph MORTON and Nancy Baker, dau. of Douglas Baker, deceased. Sur. William Scott.

20 December 1809. Joseph MORTON and Elizabeth Watkins, dau. of Thomas Watkins, deceased. Sur. Richard W. Venable. Married 21 December.

1 January 1801. Nathaniel MORTON and Betty Ann Glenn, dau. of Peyton Glenn who consents. Sur. Charles Venable. Married 15 January.

5 May 1780. Peyton MORTON and Nancy Wimbish, dau. of Elizabeth Wimbish who consents. Witness Robert Bowman. Sur. John Morrow, Jr.

10 November 1806. Robert MORTON and Marcia M. Flournoy, dau. of Thomas Flournoy, deceased. Sur. John James Flournoy. Robert son of Jacob Morton.

1 December 1803. Thomas A. MORTON and Patsy Lockett, dau. of Stephen Lockett, deceased.

16 February 1784. William MORTON and Sukey Walton, dau. of George Walton. Sur. Woodson Knight.

24 April 1784. William MORTON and Susannah Walton. (Register)

10 September 1787. William MORTON and Mary Hart, dau. of Luke Hart. Consent of Mother Mary Hart. Sur. Samuel Morton. Married 13 September.

6 December 1802. William B. MORTON and Lucy F. Flournoy, dau. of Thomas Flournoy, deceased. Sur. David Flournoy.

16 April 1801. Daniel MOSELEY and Martha Pettus, dau. of Stephen Pettus. Marriage Register.

18 May 1801. George MOSELEY and Sally Miller, dau. of John Miller, deceased. Sur. John C. Miller. Married 19 May.

19 October 1808. Samuel H. MOSES and Nancy Jennings. Marriage Register.

30 March 1802. Joseph MOTLEY and Nancy C. Childers, dau. of John Childers who consents. Sur. Absalom Farmer. Childress in Register. Married 1 April.

27 February 1806. William MOUNTCASTLE and Patsey Rice, dau. of James Rice, deceased, and Jane Rice who consents. Sur. James McDearmon. Married 1 March.

16 April 1798. George MUCKLE and Sally Caldwell, dau. of John Caldwell who is surety. Married 19 April.

20 December 1792. James MUNFORD and Martha Williams Scott. Minister's returns.

1788. Thomas MURRY and Luvenia Cannon, dau. of William Cannon.

6 November 1790. Thomas MURRAY and Susanna McCargo. Marriage Register.

21 January 1793. William NABOURS and Rosanna Meadows, dau. of Joel Meadows who consents. Sur. William Tyree. Neighbors in Register. Married 24 January.

18 June 1787. Frederick NANCE and Patsy Watkins, dau. of Henry Watkins. Sur. Joseph Scott, Jr.

8 June 1810. Abner NASH and Lucy Gaulding, dau. of Jesse Gaulding who is surety. Married 9 June 1810.

8 September 1798. Charles Fisher NASH and Judith Pankey, dau. of Stephen Pankey, Jr., deceased. Sur. Abner Nash. Married 13 September.

16 January 1805. Charles Fisher NASH and Martha Redd, dau. of John Redd who is surety. Married 17 January.

18 February 1805. John T. NASH and Susan W. Pankey, dau. of Stephen Pankey, deceased. Sur. Charles F. Nash. Married 26 February.

15 December 1801. Leban NEAL and Lucy Philips, dau. of Richard Philips who consents. Sur. Laban Hawkins.

23 February 1801. John NEALY and Nelly Harper, dau. of Edmund Harper, deceased. Sur. John Bell. Married 25 February. Neally in Register.

15 March 1788. Andrew NELSON and Mary Susannah Chambers, dau. of Josias Chambers, deceased. Consent of Mother, Mary Chambers. Sur. Abner Watson.

19 December 1791. Ashely NELSON and Mary Archdeacon, dau. of Edmund Archdeacon who is surety.

18 July 1796. John NELSON and Polly Meadows, dau. of Jeremiah Meadows who is surety.

11 October 1808. James NEVILLE and Nancy Brooks, dau. of Bartlett Brooks who is surety. Married 18 October.

16 September 1790. Soloman NEWSOM and Sarah Carrier, dau. of Henry and Mary Carrier. Sur. Samuel Cunningham.

10 March 1798. Nehemiah NOCK and Susannah Brooks, dau. of Thomas Brooks, Consent of Mother Sarah Brooks. Sur. John James.

12 March 1803. James NORTH and Patsy Elam, dau. of Joel Elam who is surety. Married 17 March.

2 October 1797. Absalom NUNNALLY and Massey Rice, dau. of Joseph Rice who consents. Sur. John Rice. Married 5 Oct.

16 May 1808. Absalom NUNNALLY and Anna Dunnivant, dau. of Dudley Dunnivant. Sur. Shadrack Dunnivant. Married 19 May 1807.

25 December 1794. Buckner NUNNALLY and Sally Rice, dau. of Joseph Rice who consents. Sur. Zachariah Rice. Buckner son of Peter Nunnally. Married 26 December.

17 October 1803. Ephraim NUNNALLY and Nancy Williamson, dau. of Thomas Williamson who is surety. Married 20 Oct.

16 November 1801. Gilliam NUNNALLY and Nancy Sadler, dau. of John Sadler who consents. Sur. Peter Nunnally. Married 19 November.

15 October 1810. James NUNNALLY and Louisa Fowlkes, dau. of John Fowlkes, deceased. Sur. William Baldwin. Married 27 October.

2 December 1807. Littleberry NUNNALLY and Mary Harper, dau. of William Harper, deceased. Sur. William Collier. Married 27 December.

5 May 1802. Peter NUNNALLY, Jr. and Dalphe Taylor Richards, dau. of John Richards who is surety. Married 6 May.

2 November 1801. John OLIVER and Sally Bradshaw, dau. of John Bradshaw, deceased and Margaret Bradshaw who consents. Sur. Richard Holt.

15 December 1806. Thomas OLIVER and Lucy Lewelling, dau. of Freeman Lewelling, deceased. Sur. John Holcomb.

6 September 1790. James OMOHUNDRO and Rosana Green, dau. of Thomas Green who consents. Sur. Ashely Johnson. Married 10 September.

16 December 1807. Richard OMOHUNDRO and Betsy Martin, dau. of Robert Martin. Sur. Henry Madison.

3 September 1783. Thomas ONNEAL and Cusey Chaffin, dau. of Standley Chaffin who consents. Sur. James Gallaspie.

4 September 1783. Thomas O'NEAL and Cuzy Chaffin. (Register)

2 July 1798. John Hendrick OSBORNE and Susanna R. Goode, dau. of Robert Goode who consents. Sur. William Goode.

18 November 1797. Skearm OSBORN and Lucy Fleming, dau. of Robert Fleming. Sur. Carter Waddell.

2 June 1779. Thomas OSBORNE and Betty Ward Estes. Sur. Abraham Estes.

26 May 1800. Moses OVERTON and Penelope Hudson, widow of Thomas Hudson. Sur. John Hudson.

11 December 1802. Richard OVERTON and Jensey Hudson, dau. of John Hudson who is surety.

5 October 1791. Archer OWEN and Lucy Kelly, dau. of William Kelly who consents. Sur. Daniel Kelly. Married 27 October. Archer Owen of Montgomery Co. See Arthur Owen.

5 October 1791. Arthur OWEN and Lucy Kelly, dau. of William Kelly who consents. Sur. Daniel Kelly. Married 27 October. Arthur Owen of Montgomery Co. See Archer Owen.

6 December 1786. Jacob OWEN and Martha Harper, dau. of Edmund Harper, deceased. Sur. Abraham Foster.

21 May 1798. Jesse OWEN and Susanna Burks, dau. of John Burks who consents. Sur. William Burks. Married 28 May.

21 January 1793. Armstead PAMPLIN and Lucy Ligon, dau. of Henry Ligon. Sur. Robert Holt.

24 October 1800. James PARIS and Sally Pindleton, dau. of Benjamin Pindleton who consents. Sur. James Dickinson.

2 June 1808. Josiah PARIS and Elizabeth Gaulding, dau. of Jesse Gaulding, who is surety.

24 May 1804. Obadiah PARIS and Judith Gaulding, dau. of Jesse Gaulding who is surety.

9 September 1794. William PATRICK and Maryann Watkins. Sur. Joel Watkins.

22 November 1792. John PATTESON and Tabitha Lovewell, dau. of Charles Lovewell who is surety.

28 September 1768. Henry PAULIN and Elizabeth Wallace, dau. of Samuel Wallace.

16 April 1804. Samuel PEARCE and Martha H. Gibson, dau. of Thomas Gibson, deceased. Sur. Robert Gibson.

10 January 1800. Charles PEEK and Nelly Brooks, dau. of Thomas Brooks, deceased. Sur. Garrett Andrews.

12 October 1805. Jesse PEEK and Ann Mitchell, dau. of James Mitchell, deceased. Sur. Thomas Shepherd.

14 December 1805. Simmons PEEK and Patsy Lancaster, dau. of Nathaniel Lancaster who consents. Sur. Robert Lancaster.

January 1794. Charles PENICK and Agnes Peek. Prince Edward Order Book Jan. Account 1794, p 106. Deed Book 10, pp. 89 - 90.

21 December 1807. Edward PENICK and Polly Jennings Hamblin, dau. of Daniel Hamblin who consents. Sur. Laban Neal. Married 24 December.

15 September 1806. Jesse PENICK and Nancy Philips, dau. of Richard Philips, deceased. Sur. Nathan Penick. Married 1 October. Jesse son of Thomas and Kesiah (Owen) Penick.

5 December 1783. (1781?). John PENICK and Prudence Rowlett, dau. of John and Edith Rowlett who consent. Sur. John Clarke, Jr. John son of John and Mary (Mallory) Penick.

29 July 1795. John PENICK and Sarah Johns, dau. of Joel Johns who consents. John son of Thomas and Kesiah (Owen) Penick.

2 May 1795. Nathaniel PENICK and Tabitha Rudd. Nathaniel son of John and Mary (Mallory) Penick.

27 August 1808. Robert PENICK and Jane Buchanan. Robert son of Charles and Agnes (Clarke) Penick.

1769. Thomas PENICK and Kesiah Owen, dau. of John and Phoebe Owen. Thomas son of John and Mary (Mallory) Penick.

1 October 1804. William PENICK and Sally Bailey, dau. of Thomas Bailey. Grandfather John Clark consents. Sur. Littleberry Clark. Married 4 October. (Thomas Baley married Milly Clark 1779.)

3 December 1798. Henry PERKINS and Elizabeth Comer Penick, dau. of Charles Penick, deceased, and Agnes Penick who consents. Sur. Thomas Tuggle. Married 5 December.

19 November 1794. Isaac PERKINS and Nancy Cawthon, dau. of Richard Cawthon, deceased. Sur. Francis Walthall. Married 20 November. See Isaac Perkinson.

10 September 1794. William PERKINS and Sarah Morton, dau. of Samuel Morton who consents. Sur. William Ransone.

19 July 1802. David PERKINSON and Martha Evans, dau. of Lud Evans. Sur. Joseph Yarborough.

20 November 1794. Isaac PERKINSON and Nancy Cawthorn. Minister's returns. See Isaac Perkins.

21 March 1791. Josiah PERKINSON and Lucy Harper. Sur. Samuel Harper.

2 November 1798. Thomas PETTUS and Ellenor Smith, dau. of William Smith. Sur. William McGehee. Married 7 November. Minister's returns say Elliner McGehee.

12 March 1781. William PETTUS (?) and Milly Watkins. Sur. Benjamin Watkins.

12 September 1801. John PHILIPS and Priscilla Beadle, dau. of Thomas Beadle. Sur. John H. Osborn.

1 October 1791. Peter T. PHILLIPS and Ann Skip Magdalean Harris, dau. of John Skip Harris, deceased. Sur. William McGehee. Married 6 October. Peter T. Phillips of Nottoway County.

1 December 1796. James PIGG and Patsey Pennill (?), dau. of Pearce B. Pennill (?). Sur. Henry Pigg.

26 September 1804. John PIGG and Sally Brown, dau. of George Brown who consents. Sur. Henry Pigg.

13 November 1792. John PILIER and Ann Berry, dau. of Joseph Berry who consents. Sur. Jonathan Mason. Register says Pillow. Married 29 November.

27 December 1797. John PILLER and Sally Vaughan, dau. of Thomas Vaughan who consents and is surety. Married 28 December.

12 December 1801. James PLANT and Patty Womack, dau. of Massanello Womack who consents. Sur. Robert Womack.

22 December 1789. Ambrose POLLARD and Mary Ann Waddle, dau. of Jacob Waddle who consents. Sur. Dennis Waddle. Ambrose Pollard of Amelia Co.

12 March 1781. William POLTOR and Milly Watkins. Sur. Benjamin Watkins. (William Poltor or Porter.)

20 May 1799. Rezin PORTER and Mary Pettus, dau. of Stephen Pettus who is surety. Married 23 May.

10 March 1791. Robert PORTER and Ann Black, dau. of James Black who consents. Sur. John Black.

9 September 1781-87. "Must have been earlier". William PORTER and Susanna Carson (Register).

24 December 1793. James POWERS and Sarah Deane Woodcock, dau. of Mark Woodcock, of Henrico Co. Sur. Richard Deane. Married 26 January.

1 November 1792. Richard POWELL and Susannah Thompson, dau. of Bartlett Thompson, deceased, of Cumberland Co. Sur. Christopher Holland.

25 November 1795. Charles P. POWERS and Betsy Dixon, dau. of John Dixon who is surety. Married 26 October(?).

25 January 1786. William PRESTON and Betsy Wood. Sur. Robert Morton.

18 October 1802. Benjamin H. PRICE and Lucy Williamson, dau. of Robert Williamson, deceased. Sur. Pugh W. Price.

2 January 1778. Bird PRICE and Elizabeth Clarke, dau. of Thomas Clarke of Hanover Co. Sur. Martin Smith.

10 November 1778. Charles PRICE and Ann Hoskins, dau. of Benjamin Hoskins who consents. Wit. Jane and Phebe Hoskins. Sur. Charles Penick.

7 September 1789. Jacob PRICE and Polly Wade, dau. of Charles Wade, deceased. Sur. Joseph Venable.

4 February 1791. James PRICE and Susannah Gilchrist. Sur. John Gilchrist. Married 7 February.

14 March 1792. Nathaniel PRICE and Frances Booker, dau. of William Booker, deceased. Mother Mary Booker. Sur. John Booker. Married 15 March.

15 February 1790. Richard PRICE and Mary Hambleton. Sur. Joseph Hambleton. Married 20 March. Register says Hamilton.

23 July 1804. Samuel PRICE and Sally Holland, dau. of Christopher H. Holland who consents. Consent of Williamson Price for Samuel. Sur. William B. Scott. Married 30 July.

28 October 17 (torn). William PRICE, Jr. and Sarah Baulding, dau. of William Baulding. Sur. Francis Watkins.

27 February 1797. Jesse PRIOR and Martha Fielder, dau. of Thomas Fielder, deceased, and Ann Fielder, who consents.

15 February 1796. Jesse PRYOR and Judith Harris, dau. of Thomas Harris, deceased. Mother Elizabeth Harris consents. Sur. Norman Peek. Married 19 February. Register says Prior.

16 February 1789. Samuel PRYOR and Fannie Ferguson, dau. of Alexander Ferguson. Sur. Samuel Greggory.

9 March 1771. David PUCKETT and Fanny Butler, dau. of Aaron Butler who is surety.

18 March 1791. Jacob PUCKETT and Nancy Woottin, dau. of Elisha Woottin who consents. Sur. Richard Gauling.

20 November 1795. James PUCKETT and Polly Franklin, dau. of Joseph Franklin who consents. Sur. William Franklin.

6 September 1797. Joel PUCKETT and Polly Young, dau. of Stephen Young who consents. Sur. Johnson Young.

26 April 1757. Peter PUCKETT and Ann Morris. Sur. William Barnet.

16 September 1781. William PUCKETT and Lucy Pendleton, dau. of Thomas Pendleton. Sur. David Puckett.

18 October 1773. George PULLIAM and Fanny Price. Sur. Williamson Byrd.

15 July 1805. George PULLIAM and Ann Penick, dau of John Penick who is surety. Minister's returns say Anna Peek.

18 October 1802. James PURCELL and Sally Goslin, dau. of John Goslin, deceased. Sur. Augustus Watson.

2 November 1787. John PURNALL and Mary Flournoy, dau. of Thomas Flournoy. Sur. Ambrose Nelson.

9 December 1780. John RAINE and Rhoda Watkins (widow?). Sur. Henry Davidson. John Raine of Cumberland Co.

8 October 1804. Charles RAINE and Nancy Elliott, widow of Andrew Elliott. Sur. William Womack, (dau. of Wm. Womack). See Charles Rains. Jr.

16 February 1789. Anthony RAINES and Mildred Burk, dau. of Richard Burk. Sur. Josiah Fowlkes.

31 August 1801. William RAINES and Patsey Baldwin, dau. of John Baldwin, deceased. Sur. Henry Baldwin. Married 3 September.

8 October 1804. Charles RAINS and Nancy Elliott. Minister's returns. See Charles Raine.

15 August 1799. William RANSOME and Susanna Dejarnette. Minister's returns. See William Ransone.

11 February 1801. Dudley RANSONE and Mary Anderson, dau. of Parsons Anderson, deceased. Sur. Hezekiah Morton. Married 12 February.

28 January 1795. John RANSONE and Patsey Penick, dau. of Charles Penick who is surety. (Martha Penick dau. Charles and Agnes Clarke Penick).

14 August 1799. William RANSONE and Susanna De Jarnette, dau. of James De Jarnette who consents. Sur. Abner Watson. Married 15 August. See William Ransome.

21 July 1788. Jesse RATHER and Fanny Dillon. Sur. John Dillon.

13 July 1791. Reuben RAY and Edy Odineal, dau. of Tyree Odineal who consents. Sur. Charles Howell. Married 18 July.

25 September 1802. Isaac READ and Anne Venable, dau. of Samuel W. Venable. Sur. Henry E. Watkins.

30 March 1782. James READ and Martha Rice, dau. of Charles Rice. Sur. Samuel Porter. See James Reid.

13 October 1800. James READ and Betsy Shepperson, dau. of Thomas Shepperson, deceased. Sur. Nathaniel Shepperson. Married 15 October.

8 July 1805. John Nash READ and Elizabeth F. Nash, dau. of John Nash, Sr., who consents. Sur. Charles F. Nash. John Nash Read of Charlotte Co. Married 9 July.

19 September 1780. John REDD and Mary Trueman, spinster. Sur. Quin Morton.

6 January 1797. John Paul REDD and Polly Tuggle, dau. of J. W. Tuggle. Sur. John Tuggle.

13 March 1798. William REDD and Betty Ann Daniel, dau. of John Daniel who is surety. Reg. says Patty Ann.

9 November 1801. Edward REDFORD and Martha V. Allen, dau. of Charles Allen. Sur. William L. Womack. Married 12 Nov. Minister's returns say Martha A. Allen.

18 February 1788. Thomas REED and Martha Black, dau. of Robert Black. Sur. William Black. Register says Reid. Married 21 February. See Thomas Reid.

4 April 1782. James REID and Martha Rice. Marriage Reg.

26 November 1788. James REID and Janey Black, dau. of Robert Black who consents. Sur. William Black. Married 2 December. Register says Jane.

5 November 1792. James REID and Nancy Young, dau. of Henry Young, deceased. Sur. Samuel Reid. Married 7 Nov.

19 May 1794. John REID and Rebecca Cawley, dau. of Barkley Cawley, deceased. Sur. William Porter. Married 22 May by Rev. William Mahon.

24 May 1766. Samuel REID and Elizabeth Shields. Sur. William Crockett.

21 February 1788. Thomas REID and Martha Black. Minister's returns. See Thomas Reed.

11 December 1807. William B. REID and Clementina Venable, dau. of Samuel W. Venable who is surety.

16 January 1809. David REYNOLDS and Mahala Wade, dau. of William Wade who consents. Sur. Robert Lancaster.

16 February 1792. John REYNOLDS and Mary Davis, dau. of Sarah Davis. Sur. Norman Peek. John son of Elkanah Reynolds.

21 December 1795. Charles RICE and Mary North. (Register).

7 February 1804. Charles RICE and Catherine Leigh dau. of John Leigh, deceased. Sur. Jeremiah Whitworth. Married 9 February.

3 February 1790. Francis RICE and Ellener Smith, widow of Jonathan Smith. Sur. Moore Weaver. Married 4 February.

7 May 1804. Isham RICE and Susanna Price, widow of James Price. Sur. Samuel Gilchrist (nee Susanna Gilchrist).

25 December 1794. John RICE and Elizabeth Talley, dau. of Tucker Talley who consents. Sur. Buckner Nunnally. John son of Joseph Rice. Married 26 December 1796.

20 October 1795. John RICE and Betty Fore, dau. of William Fore who is surety.

9 July 1802. John H. RICE and Anne Smith Morton, dau. of James Morton who is surety.

19 December 1783. Nathaniel RICE and Mary Richardson. Sur. James A. Spencer. Married 12 January 1784.

16 March 1807. Thomas RICE and Susannah Bigger, dau. of James Bigger who is surety. Married 19 March.

17 June 1789. Zachariah RICE and Elizabeth Lewis, dau. of David Lewis. Sur. John Smith.

17 December 1808. Richard RICHARDSON and Polly Elam, dau. of Joel Elam who is surety. Married 22 December. Minister's returns say Richards Richardson.

17 May 1756. John RICHIE and Jane Davis (own consent). Wit. George Davis. Sur. William Hudson.

17 December 1804. Alexander RITCHIE and Ann Watson, dau. of John Watson who consents. Sur. Drury Watson Jr. Married 20 December.

19 August 1799. Pleasant ROBERTS and Milly Owen, dau. of William Owen who consents. Sur. William Brightwell.

14 August 1804. Samuel ROBERTS and Rachel Brightwell, dau of Charles Brightwell. Sur. William Brightwell.

16 February 1789. Stephen ROBERTS and Nancy Rains, dau. of John Rains who consents. Sur. Josiah Fowlkes.

3 June 1800. Thomas ROBERTSON and Lydia Webster, dau. of Edward Webster, deceased. Sur. Townsend Wilkerson.

11 March 1777. Jesse ROBINSON and Susanna Jones. Sur. Alexander Robinson.

16 November 1792. John ROBINSON and Obedience Jackson, dau. of Joel Jackson. Sur. Robert Robinson of Amherst Co.

22 December 1792. William ROBINSON and Susanna Clarke, dau. of James Clarke who is surety. Married 25 December.

19 December 1800. Absalom ROWLAND and Oney Hurt, dau. of James Hurt who consents. Sur. Thomas Rice.

18 December 1807. Abner ROWLETT and Nancy Foster, dau. of Ezekiel Foster who is surety. Married 24 December.

17 December 1804. Jesse ROWLETT and Polly T. Owen, dau of Jesse Owen, deceased. Sur Mackness Rowlett. Married 22 Dec.

17 December 1787. John ROWLETT and Anne Owen, dau. of Jesse Owen. Sur. William Rowlett.

20 July 1791. Mackness ROWLETT and Polly Hudson, dau. of John Hudson who consents. Sur. William Rowlett.

10 July 1799. Nathan ROWLETT and Nancy Rowlett, "parent" William Rowlett (his or hers?). Sur. Daniel Worsham. William Rowlett consents.

27 March 1804. Richard ROWLETT and Nancy Mason, dau. of Joseph Mason, deceased. Sur. Simeon Walton. Married 29 March.

19 October 1807. Thomas ROWLETT and Lucy Bruce, dau. of Alexander Bruce. Sur. Thomas Penick. Married 31 October.

19 April 1785. William ROWLETT and Jemima Owen, dau. of Jesse Owen who consents. Sur. Thomas Owen. Married 21 April.

21 March 1796. John ROY and Frances Gillespie, dau. of Ann Tate. Consent of Samuel and Anne Tate. Sur. Philip Taggart. Married 7 April.

20 April 1782. John RUDD and Agnes Clarke. (Register)

31 December 1795. John RUDD and Sarah Johns, dau. of John Johns, deceased. Sur. Leonard Sibley.

15 June 1801. John RUDD and Mary Perkinson, widow of William Perkinson. Sur. Thomas Pettus. Married 17 June.

6 October 1804. Wiley RUSSELL and Polly Gaulding, dau. of Alexander Gaulding who is surety. Wyley in Register.

29 August 1793. Joseph RUTLEDGE and Anne Atwood, dau. of James Atwood.

13 July 1805. Peter RUTLEDGE and Elizabeth Bean, widow of William Bean. Sur. John Boyns.

18 August 1794. William RUTLEDGE and Martha Chumbley, dau. of John Chumbley, deceased. Sur. William Singleton. Married 20 October 1796.

25 December 1807. John W. RYE and Elizabeth Lowe, dau. of David Lowe who is surety.

19 August 1805. Thomas SADLER and Delila King, dau. of William King, deceased. Sur. Emanuel J. Leigh.

3 February 1792. William J. SADLER and Betsy Roberts, dau. of Henry Roberts who consents. Sur. Alexander Gaulding. Married 4 February.

9 April 1805. Francis SANDERS and Sally B. Penick, dau. of William and Judith Penick. Sur. William Penick. Minister's returns say Sarah Penick.

16 December 1805. James SANDERS and Nancy T. Tuggle, dau. of Thomas Tuggle who is surety. Married 19 December.

23 December 1797. John SANDERS and Judith Fore. Minister's returns. See John Saunders.

18 December 1797. John SAUNDERS and Judith Fore, dau. of William Fore who is surety. Married 23 December. See John Sanders.

12 September 1786. Robert SAUNDERS and Sally Chappell, dau. of Robert Chappell who consents. Sur. William Fair.

30 January 1804. Thomas SAUNDERS and Hope Ann Penick, dau. of William Penick who is surety. Married 2 February. (Hope Ann dau. of William and Judith Penick.)

19 February 1798. Benjamin SCOTT and Sarah Legrand, dau. of Alexander Legrand who is surety. Married 8 March.

21 May 1798. Edward F. SCOTT and Elizabeth Redd, dau. of George Redd who is surety. Married 29 May.

14 December 1792. James SCOTT and Elizabeth Cunningham, dau. of Alexander Cunningham. Sur. Jacob Cunningham. Married 17 December.

18 November 1806. Samuel SCOTT and Elizabeth H. C. Bigger, dau. of John Bigger who is surety. Consent of William Scott as to Samuel Scott.

3 June 1801. Thomas SCOTT and Jane Haskins, dau. of Thomas Haskins who is surety. Married 11 June.

10 October 1781. William SCOTT and Mary Baker. (Register).

18 December 1782. William SCOTT and Mary Baker, widow of Douglas Baker. Sur. Andrew Elliott.

21 January 1805. Nathan SCRUGGS and Rhoda Wooldridge, dau. of Simon Wooldridge. Sur. James Paris.

1 August 1807. John SEAY and Patsy Akin, dau. of Charles Akin, deceased. Consent of guardian Josiah Perkinson. Sur. William Fisher. Married 6 August.

9 August 1810. William SEAY and Susan T. Hopkins, dau. of Joseph Hopkins, deceased. Sur. Moses Tredway. Minister's returns say Susan S. Hopkins.

15 March 1806. Charles SELBY and Martha Farmer, dau. of Forrest Farmer, deceased. Consent of her Mother, Ruth Fielder. Sur. Littleberry Farmer. See Charles Silvey.

20 October 1800. John SELBY and Sally Lowdon, widow of Benjamin Lowdon. Sur. Thomas Gibbons. (Benjamin Lowdon and Sarah Gibbons, dau. of John Gibbons, deceased. 15 September 1794.) Married 23 October. See John Silby.

19 March 1793. Samuel SELBY and Polly Gibbons, dau. of John Gibbons, deceased. Sur. Peter Gibbons. Married 21 April. Minister's returns say Mary Gibbons.

15 November 1790. William SELBY and Fanny Davis, dau. of William Davis who consents. Sur. Peter Gallahorn. Married 16 November. See William Silby.

7 October 1805. Robert SELF and Patsy Walker, dau. of William Walker, deceased. Sur. Alexander LeGrand, Jr.

16 May 1785. Josiah SHARP and Mary Berry, dau. of Joseph Berry who is surety. Married 18 May. Minister's returns say 1784.

20 February 1809. Leonard SHEFFIELD and Lucy C. Wootten, dau. of Jesse Wootten. Sur. Anderson P. Miller. Married 23 February. Register says Lucy O.

8 March 1785. George SHELLIDY and Jane Graham. (Register.)

11 December 1784. Young SHELTON and Henrietta Shelton, dau. of James Shelton who consents. Sur. Benjamin Mason.

2 December 1790. Samuel SHEPARD and Jenny Guill. Sur. Thomas Shephard. Married 23 December.

26 March 1799. William SHEPHERD and Elizabeth S. Allen, dau. of James Allen who is surety. Married 28 March.

5 May 1798. Benjamin SHEPPARD and Mary Hurt, dau. of Benjamin Hurt, deceased. Guardian, Massanello Womack, consents. Sur. David Thackston. Married 10 May. Judith in Register.

10 May 1798. Benjamin SHEPPARD and Judith Hurt. Minister's returns.

30 September 1794. Thomas SHEPPARD and Easter Simmons, dau. of John Simmons who consents. Sur. James Thackston.

14 January 1800. Thomas SHEPPARD and Hetty Peek, dau. of Henry Peek who consents. Sur. Jeffrey Peek. Married 16 Jan.

28 March 1799. William SHEPPARD and Elizabeth S. Allen. Minister's returns.

4 May 1796. Nathaniel SHEPPERSON and Jane Caldwell, dau. of James Caldwell who consents. Sur. Tarlton Woodson. Married 19 May.

6 July 1810. Nathaniel SHEPPERSON and Nancy Morgan, dau. of Thomas Morgan who is surety. Married 16 June.

10 October 1783. John SHIELDS and Isabel Cole. Son of Patrick Shields who consents. Manassas McFeely consents for Isabel Cole.

23 October 1800. John SILBY and Sally London. Minister's returns. See John Selby.

16 November 1790. William SILBY and Fanny Davis. Minister's returns. See William Selby.

18 May 1792. John SILVEA and Martha Muraine, dau. of Lawrence Muraine, deceased. Consent of mother, Masdry Muraine. Sur. Absalom Fear.

16 March 1806. Charles SILVEY and Martha Farmer. Minister's returns. See Charles Selby.

27 October 1801. William Alexander SIMPSON and Jerusha Marsh, dau. of Zophar Marsh who is surety. Married 29 October.

30 November 1781. Richard SLYTHE and Elizabeth Vaughan. (Register.)

17 December 1804. Allen SMITH and Mary Watson, dau. of John Watson, Jr. Sur. Drury Watson, Jr. Married 20 Dec.

10 April 1786. Edward SMITH and Margaret Graham (Register.)

19 August 1782. Francis SMITH and Martha Allen, dau. of James Allen who is surety.

11 July 1786. George SMITH and Mary Graham, dau. of Thomas Graham who consents. Sur. James Graham. George Smith of Montgomery Co. Married   September.

14 October 1793. George SMITH and Elizabeth Barksdale, dau. of Dudley Barksdale who is surety. Married 17 October.

18 November 1765. John Pemberton SMITH and Susanna Burks. Sur. George Burks.

19 August 1767. John SMITH and Susanna Watson, dau. of John Watson who is surety. John Smith of Amelia Co.

5 April 1779. John Blair SMITH and Elizabeth Fisher Nash, dau. of John Nash. Sur. Francis Watkins. Wit. David McBride.

19 December 1793. Joseph SMITH and Elizabeth Black, dau. of James Black. Sur. John Black. Joseph Smith of Campbell Co.

22 December 1804. Joseph W. SMITH and Elizabeth Burks, dau. of John Burks who consents and is surety.

16 August 1805. Martin P. SMITH and Polly Williamson, dau. of Robert Williamson, deceased. Sur. Benjamin Watkins. Married 21 August.

7 November 1799. Paton SMITH and Elizabeth Dunnivant, dau. of Clem Dunnivant, deceased. Sur. Walthall Marshall.

13 November 1803. Pemberton SMITH and Polly Thackston, dau. of James Thackston, deceased. Sur. John McGehee. Married 15 November.

17 July 1809. Richard SMITH and Tabitha Smith, dau. of Owen Smith who consents. Sur. John P. Smith. Married 20 July.

21   1789. Robert SMITH and Rebecca Booker, dau. of William Booker, deceased. Sur. John Purnall.

18 June 1804. Sterling SMITH and Mary H. Philips, dau. of Richard Philips who is surety. Married 21 June.

23 November 1804. William T. SMITH and Elizabeth Fuqua, dau. Giles Fuqua who consents. Sur. James Dillon. Married 27 November.

9 April 1782. Philemon SOUTHERLAND and Fanny Penick, dau. of William and Judith (Pate?) Penick. Sur. William Penick.

8 March 1784. John SPAULDING and Judith Burton, dau. of Samuel Burton who consents. Sur. Josiah Gaulding. Married 9 March. Minister's returns say Benton.

6 November 1783. James SPENCER and Betty Ann Richerson (Register).

4 November 1783. James Anderson SPENCER and Betty Ann Richardson, dau. of Isham Richardson who consents. Sur. John Richardson.

7 September 1786. Samuel F. SPENCER and Agnes Morton, dau. of Thomas Morton who consents. Sur. Joseph Morton.

27 December 1787. Daniel STAMPER and Sally Griffith, dau. of William Griffith who is surety.

5 October 1809. Thomas STANLEY and Nancy Giles, dau. of William Giles who is surety.

4 August 1796. Charles STAPLES and Priscilla Baugh, dau. of John Baugh, deceased. Consent of guardian Thomas Trent. Sur. Hobson Hood.

4 February 1803. William STEGER and Polly Bigger, dau. of John Bigger, Sr., who consents. Sur. Wiltshire Cardwell.

7 September 1784. John STION and Cressy Womack, dau. of Mather Womack who consents. Wit. Alexander Gordon and Claberne Scott.

15 January 1787. Jacob St. JOHN and Agnes Johnson, dau. of Edward Johnson, deceased. Sur. William Smith. Married 16 January.

20 April 1807. William W. SUDBERRY and Oney Rudd, dau. of John Rudd who is surety. Married 7 May.

25 July 1805. John SUMPTER and Hannah Morrison, dau. of Samuel Morrison who is surety. Married 27 July.

7 December 1802. John TAGGART and Janey Caldwell, dau. of John Caldwell who consents. Sur. George Mickle. Married 9 December. Minister's returns say Jane.

19 December 1803. Martin TAGGART and Sarah Hurt, dau. of Benjamin Hurt, deceased. Guardian, Massanello Womack, consents. Sur. Benjamin Sheppard.

9 February 1791. Robert TALLEY and Rachel Rice. (Register).

5 April 1799. Robert TARPLEY and Jency Gears, dau. of Thomas Gears who is surety.

29 May 1792. William TARPLEY and Mary Oliver, dau. of John Oliver, deceased. Consent of mother Lydia Oliver. Consent of guardian John Tarpley for William Tarpley. Sur. Christopher Dejarnett.

6 December 1791. Samuel TATE and Anne Gillespie, dau.? of William Gillespie, deceased. Sur. Philip McTaggart. Married 8 December. (I think she was widow of William Gillespie. See marriage of John Roy and Frances Gillespie).

9 January 1808. James TATUM and Sarah Morgan, dau. of Jehu Morgan who consents. Sur. James Traylor. Married 10 January.

25 April 1807. John W. TAYLOR and Polly Cooke, who is 21, dau. of John Cooke, deceased. Consent of mother Mary Cooke. Sur. Elisha Owen. Married 28 April.

16 December 1778. John TEBBS and Penelope Buxton. Sur. William Watkins.

12 September 1785. Henry TERRY and Mary Ann Baldwin, dau. of Thomas Baldwin who consents. Sur. Caleb Baldwin. Married 21 November.

5 February 1782. Ben THACKSTON and Elizabeth Ann Chambers, dau. of Josiah Chambers who consents. Sur. Charles Allen. Married 7 Feb.

5 November 1792. James THACKSTON Jr. and Frances Simmons, dau. of John Simmons who consents. Sur. David Thackston. Married 8 November. Minister's returns say Frances Woodall.

8 January 1765. James THACKSTON and Sarah Elebank (widow). Sur. John Bigger.

24 January 1794. John THACKSTON and Nancy Wilkerson, dau. of Lovel Wilkerson who consents. Sur. William Thackston.

14 November 1785. Nathaniel THACKSTON and Elizabeth Foster, dau. of Richard Foster who is surety. Married 21 November.

6 January 1798. Nathaniel THACKSTON and Francis S Andrews, dau. of John Andrews Sr. who consents. Sur. Samuel W. Venable.

8   1792. James THAXTON and Frances Woodall.(Register)

21 December 1785. William THAXTON and Lucy Guill.

2 November 1803. William THAXTON and Katherine Tate, dau. of Samuel and Mary Tate who consent. Sur. John Taggart. Minister's returns say married 30 April 1803, also Catherine and Thackston.

        1794. Zadok B. THACKSTON and Susanna Paylor, dau. of William Paylor, deceased.

20 April 1786. Peter THOMAS and Anne Mills. Sur. James McDowell.

19 January 1803. Philip THOMAS and Patsy Fuqua, dau. of Joseph Fuqua who consents and is surety.

1 January 1800. Arnold THOMASON, Jr. and Sally Rice, dau. of James Rice who is surety.

5 January 1796. Jesse THOMASON and Avey Davidson, dau. of William Davidson who consents. Sur. John Davidson.

4 September 1786. Alexander THOMPSON and Margaret Ritchie, dau. of John Ritchie, deceased. Consent of Mother, Jane Ritchie. Margaret is 21. Sur. Alexander Ritchie. Married 7 December.

3 September 1792. Andrew THOMPSON and Isabell Black, dau. of James Black who consents. Sur. John Black. Andrew Thompson of Campbell Co. Married 6 September.

7 January 1797. Carter THOMPSON and Nancy Morton, dau. of John Morton, deceased. Sur. Hezekiah Morton. Married 12 Jan.

20 August 1797. James THOMPSON and Sally Baker, widow of Douglas Baker. Sur. John Hix.

Before September 1786. John THOMPSON and Elizabeth (Eleanor?) Barton.

5 January 1792. Robert THOMPSON and Elizabeth Hamilton. Register.

3 January 1792. Robert THOMPSON and Elizabeth Reed, dau. of Robert Reed who consents. Sur. Caleb Baker.

. Thomas THOMPSON and Nancy Weddill Carter, dau. of Theodrick Carter. Sur. Thomas Carter.

19 November 1793. William THOMPSON and Elizabeth Grissell, dau. of Henry Grissell. Sur. Dick Holland.

18 February 1808. William J. THORNTON and Elizabeth G. Baker, dau. of Caleb Baker, deceased. Sur. Samuel Allen, Jr.

20 June 1798. John THURMAN and Doshea Hill, dau. of William Hill who is surety. Married 23 June.

17 October 1785. Richard THURMOND and Judith Zachary, dau. of Bartholomew Zachary who consents. Sur. William Tyree.

16 December 1778. John TIBBS and Penelope Buxton. Sur. William Watkins.

15 February 1804. Major TINSLEY and Elizabeth Owen, dau. of Elisha Owen who is surety.

17 November 1786. William TINSLEY and Susannah Morton, dau. of Richard Morton who is surety.

25 November 1807. Charles TODD and Sally Dick. Minister's returns. See Christopher Todd.

23 November 1807. Christopher TODD and Sally Dick, dau. of James Dick, Sr. Sur. Nathanial Dick. See Charles Todd.

5 March 1796. George TOMBS and Elizabeth Carter. Minister's returns. See George Toombs.

17 May 1798. William TOMBS and Sally Hamlett. Minister's returns. See William Toombs.

2 March 1796. George TOOMBS and Elizabeth Carter, dau. of William Carter who consents, and is surety. See George Tombs.

12 May 1798. William TOOMBS and Sally Hamlett, dau. of David Hamlett who is surety. Married 17 May. See William Tombs.

20 August 1781. James TRABUE and Jane Ewing Porter, Sur. Andrew Porter. Married 23 August.

9 January 1790. Alexander TRENT and Frances McTaggart, dau. of Philip McTaggart who is surety.

29 April 1808. Alexander TRENT and Jensey Carter, dau. of Daniel Carter, deceased. Sur. Povall Carter. Married 30 April. Register says Janey.

19 October 1796. James TUGGLE and Nancy Morris, dau. of John Morris, deceased. Sur. John Tuggle. Married 20 Oct.

13 March 1781. Thomas TUGGLE and Nancy Penick, dau. of William and Judith (Pate?) Penick. Sur. William Penick. Married 15 March.

9 February 1791. Robert TURNER and Elizabeth Attwell, dau. of John and Mary Attwell who consent. Sur. George Attwell.

4 January 1792. Stephen Dickerson TURNER and Phebe Ligon, dau. of Harry Ligon, deceased, and Elizabeth Ligon. Sur. Robert Holt. Married 5 January. Stephen D. Turner of Charlotte Co. and son of Keziah Turner.

29 April 1800. David TYREE and Betty Hill, dau. of John Hill who consents. Sur. Caleb Baldwin. Married 1 May. Minister's returns say Elizabeth Hill.

12 January 1793. Benjamin VAN AMBURGH and Betsy Price, widow of Charles Price. Sur. Tarlton Woodson.

14 October 1789. James VASS and Sarah Holt, dau. of Mary Holt. Sur. John Holt.

19 December 1795. Claiborne VAUGHAN and Mary Ferguson, dau. of Richard Ferguson who is surety.

20 September 1790. James VAUGHAN and Sarah Mason. Sur. William Hawkins.

9 February 1792. John VAUGHAN and Betsy Nelson, dau. of Henry Nelson who is surety. Married 11 February.

12 May 1810. Jack VAUGHAN and Nancy Haskins. Minister's returns.

7 February 1793. Richard VAUGHAN and Drusilla Rice, dau. of Matthew Rice who consents. Sur. Zachariah Rice.

19 November 1798. Richard VAUGHAN and Mary Ann Jackson, widow of Isaiah Jackson. Sur. Zachariah Rice. Married 1 December.

18 December 1809. William K. VAUGHAN and Elizabeth Glenn, dau. of Daniel Glenn, who is surety.

21 September 1801. Abraham VENABLE and Elizabeth Taylor, dau. of Joseph Taylor who consents. Sur. Blake B. Woodson.

6 February 1807. John H. VENABLE and Dorothy Glenn, dau. of Peyton Glenn who consents. Sur. James Madison. Edward Redford, guardian of John H. Venable, consents. Married 11 February.

20 January 1791. Joseph VENABLE and Elizabeth Watkins. (Register.)

16 December 1799. Josiah VENABLE and Jane C. Thornton, dau. of Sterling C. Thornton who is surety.

24 March 1755. Nathaniel VENABLE and Elizabeth Woodson. Sur. Abraham Venable.

25 February 1799. Nathaniel VENABLE, Jr. and Martha Venable, Son of Nathaniel Venable, Sr. who consents. Sur. Frank Watkins. Married 28 February.

19 September 1796. Robert VENABLE and Judith Pate Jackson, dau. of Matthew Jackson. Sur. Jacob Venable. Married 22 December.

18 February 1782. Richard VERNON and Esther Hambleton, dau. of Alexander Hambleton who is surety. Married 28 Feb.

5 January 1792. Robert VERNON and Elizabeth Hambleton, dau. of Alexander Hambleton. Sur. James Hambleton. Married 19 January. Hamilton in Register.

2 December 1790. Charles WADDELL and Nancy Marshall. Minister's returns. See Charles Waddle.

8 April 1796. Edward WADDELL and Nancy Osborne, dau. of Samuel Osborne who is surety.

20 December 1802. Carter WADDELL and Frances Armes, dau. of John Armes, who is surety. Married 23 December.

4 September 1789. Dennis WADDELL and Elizabeth Haskins, Sur. Laban Hawkins.

12 November 1788. Jacob WADDELL and Sarah Hawkins, widow of Joseph Hawkins. Sur. Fr. Watkins. Married 30 October.

27 October 1802. John WADDELL and Patience Marshall, dau. of Alexander Marshall. John son of William Waddell. Sur. Walthall Marshall.

14 March 1810. Thomas WADDELL and Barshala Akin, dau. of Charles Akin, deceased. Guardian Josiah Perkinson, consents. Sur. William Fleming. Register says Basheba Aken. Married 15 March.

14 December 1801. Walker WADDELL and Susan Smith, dau. of Owen Smith, who consents. Sur. Matthew Branch. Married 17 December. Minister's returns say Susanna.

13 May 1787. William WADDELL and Mary Sheppard, dau. of Isaac Sheppard. William son of Richard Waddell who consents. Sur. Fr. Watkins. Married 17 May.

15 November 1790. Charles WADDLE and Nancy Marshall. Sur. Alexander Marshall. Married 2 December. See Charles Waddel

2 February 1790. Nathaniel WADDLE and Mary Dunnavant. Sur. Dennis Waddell. Nathaniel Waddle of Halifax Co.

10 December 1799. Anderson WADE and Milly Wade Carter, dau. of Waddill Carter, deceased. Robert Anderson states she is his step-daughter and is surety. Married 13 December. (Robert Anderson married 19 April 1790. Mildred Carter, widow of Waddle Carter.)

14 September 1785. Daniel WADE and Lucy Davis Green, dau. of Thomas Green who consents. Sur. Parrish Green. Married 15 September.

7 January 1795. Hampton WADE and Elizabeth Green, dau. of Thomas Green who consents. Sur. Thomas Fears. Married 8 Jan.

5 June   . William WALKER and Lucy Williams. Sur. Samuel Williams. John LeNeve, Clerk.

21 March 1785. William WALKER and Mary Ann Smith, dau. of John Smith who is surety. Married - July 1785.

22 December 1806. William WALKER and Frances Sweeny, dau. of John Sweeny who consents. Sur. James Crews. Married 25 December.

9 July 1796. William WALLACE and Masdoe Shewmaker, dau. of Lande Shewmaker who consents. Sur. John Silver. Married 4 July. Mardie Shoemaker in Register.

22 November 1802. Branch WALTHALL and Anne D. Miller, dau. of John Miller, deceased. Sur. Anderson P. Miller.

31 October 1796. Francis WALTHALL and Sally Spencer, dau. of Sharp Spencer who is surety. Married 3 November.

14 February 1803. Francis M. WALTHALL and Elizabeth Foster, dau. of George Foster who consents. Sur. John Haskins. Married 18 February.

21 May 1810. Henry WALTHALL and Harriet H. Perkinson, dau. of Josiah Perkinson who is surety. Married 23 May.

23 December 1805. George WALTON and Polly Smith, dau. of Henry Smith who is surety.

18 April 1784. John WALTON and Doshea Walton, dau. of George Walton who consents. Married 22 January 1784. Sur. Thomas Walton, Sr. George Walton's will 1796 mentions dau. Doshea and son-in-law John Walton "moved to Georgia."

25 January 1791. Matthew WALTON and Frances Watkins, dau. of Henry Watkins. Sur. Robert Watkins.

19 December 1791. Simeon WALTON and Jemima Wootten, dau. of William Wootten who consents. Sur. Samuel Wootten. Simeon Walton of Nottoway Co.

16 February 1801. Simeon WALTON and Judith McGehee, dau. of William McGehee who consents. Sur. Thomas Pettus. Married 26 February.

5 July 1786. James WARE and Elizabeth Miller, dau. of John Miller who consents. Sur. Andrew Ware. Married 22 Sept.

6 May 1791. Walter WARFIELD and Sarah Winston Christian. Sur. Peter Johnston.

4 February 1805. Benjamin WATKINS and Susannah Dupuy, dau. of John Dupuy who consents. Sur. James L. Campbell. Married 7 February.

9 January 1765. Francis WATKINS and Agnes Woodson, dau. of Richard Woodson who is surety. Francis son of Thomas Watkins who consents.

26 November 1803. Francis WATKINS, Jr. and Ann N. Haskins, dau. of Thomas Haskins. Sur. Thomas C. Scott.

30 September 1786. George WATKINS and Ann Redd, dau. of Thomas Redd. Sur. William Major. Married 12 January 1787.

7 November 1808. Joel WATKINS and Polly Hill, dau. of William Hill who consents. Sur. Samuel Watkins.

16 April 1810. Silas WATKINS and Lucy M. Clark, dau. of Thomas Clark, deceased. Guardian John Clark, consents and is surety. Married 26 April.

4 April 1782. Thomas WATKINS and Betsy Ann Venable, dau. of Nathaniel Venable who consents. Sur. Abr. B. Venable. Married 2 July.

6 February 1762. Thomas WATKINS and Sally Walton. Guardian, George Walton consents.

4 December 1799. William M. WATKINS and Elizabeth W. Venable, dau. of Samuel W. Venable who consents. Married 6 December.

5 October 1803. Benjamin WATSON and Disey Dejarnett, dau. of Bowler Dejarnett, deceased. Sur. Francis Jackson.

3 August 1761. Douglas WATSON and Margaret Parks. Sur. Peter Le Grand.

25 July 1809. Enoch WATSON and Susannah Hill, dau. of John Hill, Sr. who consents. Sur. William Hill. Married 29 July.

10 December 1790. Jesse WATSON and Dolly Meredith, dau. of Pleasant Meredith of Henrico Co. who consents. Sur. Francis Watkins. Her name corrected to Polly.

17 December 1799. Samuel WATSON Jr. and Hannah Watson. Samuel Watson Jr. son of Samuel Watson Sr. who is surety.

10 April 1767. William WATSON and Jean Baker, widow. Sur. John Le Neve.

5 September 1789. William WEAKLEY and Magdaline Burton. Sur. Josiah Burton.

26 July 1796. John WEAVER and Betsy Claiborne, dau. of George Claiborne who is surety.

19 December 1804. Samuel WEAVER and Sally Wilson, dau. of Joseph Wilson who is surety.

20 December 1802. Thomas WEAVER and Mary McGehee, dau. of William McGehee who consents. Sur. Abraham McGehee. Married 23 December.

1 October 1803. Daniel WEBB and Polly Gilliam, dau. of James Gilliam who consents. Sur. John Gilliam.

2 April 1798. Simeon WEBBER and Sally Jackson, dau. of James Jackson who is surety. Married 8 April.

18 October 1798. John WEBSTER and Sally (Polly?) Cawthorn, dau. of John Cawthorn, deceased. John Webster 21 on 8 October. Sur. Thomas Wilkerson.

    1784. James WELSH and Anne (?) Chaffin (Register).

13 October 1804. Reuben WEST and Polly Brown, dau. of Wilson Brown, deceased. Sur. Elliott Baker. Married 15 October.

25 March 1785. Amos WESTBROOK and Elizabeth Palmer, dau. of Reuben Palmer who consents Sur. William Palmer.

30 July 1793. William WHITAKER and Frances Lawrence. Minister's returns. See William Whitteker.

20 December 1790. Anderson WHITE and Jane Armstrong, Sur. John Armstrong. Register says Jane Andrews. Married 3 January 1791.

Samuel WHITE and Elizabeth Smith, dau. of George Smith who is surety.

21 December 1801. William S. WHITE and Frances Childress, widow of William Childress. Sur. Zach Rice.

20 January 1800. John WHITEHEAD and Martha Baker, dau. of Samuel Baker who consents. Sur. John Baker. Married 22 January.

18 April 1808. William WHITLOW and Martha B. C. Ward, dau. of Robert Ward, deceased. Sur. Daniel Williams. Married 26 February 1809. See William Whitton.

30 July 1793. William WHITTEKER and Frances Lawrence, widow of John Lawrence, deceased. Sur. George King. See William Whitaker.

26 February 1809. William WHITTON and Martha C. B. Ward. Minister's returns. See William Whitlow.

2 November 1780. Drury WILKERSON and Mary Rice. Marriage register.

15 December 1800. George WILKERSON and Elizabeth Caldwell, dau. of John Caldwell who is surety.

12 March 1793. John WILKERSON and Tabitha Johnson, dau. of William Johnson who consents. Sur. Towson Wilkerson. Married 14 March.

15 March 1805. John WILKERSON and Betsy Franklin, dau. of Thomas Franklin who consents. Sur. John Preston. Married 16 March.

16 September 1807. John WILKERSON and Lucy Penick, dau. of Thomas Penick who is surety. Married 24 September. Lucy, dau. of Thomas and Kesiah (Owen) Penick.

20 December 1799. Nathaniel WILKERSON and Elizabeth Thaxton, dau. of David Thaxton who consents. Consent of Towson Wilkerson for his son Nathaniel. Sur. Robert Thaxton. Married 26 December.

29 October 1796. Thomas WILKERSON and Elizabeth Farmer, dau. of Elmer Farmer, deceased and of Ruth Farmer. Sur. Towson Wilkerson. Married 10 November.

2 August 1802. Turner WILKERSON and Agnes Brooks, dau. of Thomas Brooks, deceased. Sur. Arter Conner. Married 3 Aug.

2 November 1780. Drury WILKINSON and Mary Rice. (Register).

9 January 1784. Sherwood WILKINSON and Peggy Morrow. (Register).

21 December 1803. William WILKINSON and Elizabeth A. Smith, dau. of Francis Smith who consents. Sur. Thomas C. Scott.

30 January 1799. Abner WILLARD and Sally Roberts, dau. of Henry Roberts who consents. Sur. Richard Goulding. Married 31 January.

18 May 1756. John WILLARD and Marth Edwards, dau. of Simon Edwards who consents. Sur. Thomas Turpin.

5 January 1791. Nixon WILLARD and Sarah Robertson. Sur. Isaac Robertson.

21 March 1782. William WILLIARD and Mary Barnett. Marriage Register. Minister's say married 27 March.

25 August 1790. William WILLARD and Sally Gaulding. Sur. William Nixon.

6 August 1780. Thomas WILLIAMS Jr. and Esther Morrow. Sur. Roger Williams.

7 January 1789. William WILLIAMS and Eleanor Porter, dau. of Andrew Porter who consents. Sur. Robert Porter.

26 November 1804. John WILLIAMSON and Martha Nunnally, dau. of Peter Nunnally who consents. Sur. Benjamin Nunnally. Consent of Thomas Williamson father of John. Married 1 December.

18 May 1756. John WILLIARD and Martha Edwards, dau. of Simon Edwards who consents. Sur. Thomas Turpin.

4 November 1802. Goodridge WILSON and Elizabeth Venable, dau of Nathaniel Venable who consents. Sur. Alexander Wilson.

18 September 1780. John WILSON and Elizabeth Moore, dau. of John Moore who consents. Sur. Andrew Baker.

6 March 1794. John WILSON and Martha Bracher, dau. of John Bracher, deceased and Margaret Bracher. Sur. Thomas Wingo.

9 February 1803. Stephen WILSON and Rebecca Massey, dau. of Sherwood Massey, deceased. Sur. Stephen Howell. Married 10 February.

20 February 1789. Thomas WILSON and Elizabeth Burton, dau. of Samuel Burton who consents. Sur. Robert Burton.

19 September 1797. Thomas WILSON and Elizabeth Worsham, dau. of Charles Worsham who is surety. Married 25 Sept.

2 July 1800. Thomas WILSON and Rebecca Carr, dau. of Hugh Carr, deceased. Consent of Ann Carr. Sur. John Cunningham. Married 4 July.

21 April 1792. William WILSON and Frankie Sheperd, dau. of Robert Shepherd who consents. Sur. Samuel Sheperd.

23 May 1763. Samuel WIMBISH and Mildred Martin, dau. of John Martin who consents. Sur. James Thackston.

16 June 1791. Jesse WINFREE and Frances A. Spencer, dau. of John Spencer who consents. Sur. Robert Watkins.

8 May 1792. William WINGO and Fanny Shepard. Marriage Register.

25 December 1795. Peter WINN and Frances Akin, dau. of Charles Akin, deceased. Sur. Simeon Walton.

16 October 1809. Richard WINN and Susan P. Mathews, dau. of William Mathews, deceased. Sur. William T. Walker.

25 December 1798. Alexander WOMACK and Sarah McDearman, dau. of Dudley McDearman. Sur. William Davis. Married 27 December.

28 November 1805. Anthony WOMACK and Prudence Branch, dau. of Mathew Branch, Sr. Sur. Mathew Branch, Jr. Married 29 November.

21 November 1797. Archer WOMACK and Ann Farish Flournoy, dau. of Thomas Flournoy who is surety.

1 April 1799. Charles WOMACK and Patsy Womack, dau. of William Womack Sr. who is surety.

10 February 1775. Massanello WOMACK and Elizabeth Venable, dau. of Charles Venable. Sur. John Holcombe.

17 November 1806. Robert V. WOMACK and Martha Glenn, dau. of Peyton Glenn who is surety. Married 26 November.

7 July 1795. Tignal WOMACK and Nancy Meadows? Rudder, dau. of Samuel Rudder, deceased. Consent of guardian, Burwell Brown. Sur. Archer Womack. Married 8 July.

14 March 1808. William L. WOMACK and Mary C. Venable, dau. of Samuel W. Venable. Sur. William T. Reid. Minister's returns say married 2 November 1809.

14 February 1787. Carlos WOOD and Priscilla Holloway, dau. of John Holloway who consents. Sur. Samuel C. LeNeve. See Carolus Wood.

15 January 1787. Carolus WOOD and Priscilla Holloway. Minister's returns. See Carlos Wood.

9 February 1785. John WOOD and Anne Hundley, dau. of George Hundley, deceased, and Anne Hundley who consents. Sur. Stephen Wood.

18 December 1806. Robert WOOD and Elizabeth Hurt, dau. of Obadiah Hurt who consents. Sur. John Wood.

13 September 1809. Thomas WOOD, Jr. and Sally Arnold, dau. of John Arnold who consents. Sur. David Arnold. Thomas Wood, Jr. of Buckingham Co.

15 December 1800. Isaac WOODALL and Nancy Ferguson, dau. of John Ferguson, deceased. Sur. Elijah Maddox.

1 November 1785. Jacob WOODALL and Frances Simmons, dau. of John Simmons who consents. Sur. Nathaniel Simmons.

10 January 1797. James WOODALL and Betsy Taylor, dau. of James Taylor. Sur. Mumford DeJarnett.

12 March 1798. William WOODALL and Judith Self. Sur. John Fielder.

8 January 1802. William WOODALL and Rebecca Robertson, dau. of Jesse Robertson who is surety.

21 March 1804. William WOODALL and Susannah Gaulding, dau. of Alexander Gaulding, deceased. Sur. Richard Gaulding.

March 1792. John WOODFIN and Nancy Pulliam, dau. of John Pulliam. Sur. John Smith. Married 22 March.

10 June 1795. Micajah WOODS and Lucy Walker, dau. of Henry Walker, deceased. Sur. Benjamin Burton. Consent of guardian, John A. Jones. Married 13 August.

13 September 1797. Stephen WOODRUM and Peggy Porter, dau. of Andrew Porter. Sur. William Mitchell.

Jacob WOODSON and Elizabeth Morton, dau. of John Morton who is surety.

18 August 1800. John W. WOODSON and Susanna Gilliam, dau. of James Gilliam who consents. Sur. John Gilliam. Married 11 September.

12 April 1803. Obadiah WOODSON and Mary Watson, dau. of Drury Watson. Sur. Drury Watson, Jr.

20 November 1792. William WOODSON and Ann Lancaster, dau. of Nathaniel Lancaster. Sur. Charles Fore. Married 29 November.

6 January 1795. Benjamin WOOSLEY and Nancy Meadows, dau. of Joel Meadows, deceased, of Amelia Co. Sur. Archibald Meadows of Amelia Co.

21 December 1807. William T. WOOTTON and Elizabeth Perkinson, dau. of William Perkinson, deceased. William T. Wootton son of William Wootton. Sur. Archibald Fuqua. Married 24 December.

21 January 1788. Charles WORSHAM and Mary Chappell Ellington, dau. David Ellington who is surety. Charles Worsham of Amelia Co. Married 25 January.

15 March 1776. Daniel WORSHAM and Ellen Leigh, dau. of John Leigh. Sur. Paschal Greenhill. Daniel son of Thomas Worsham who consents. Daniel Worsham of Chesterfield Co.

22 November 1798. William WORSHAM and Dicey Holt, dau. of David Holt who is surety.

27 December 1808. William H. WORSHAM and Elizabeth Price, dau. of Jacob Price who is surety.

20 November 1764. Thomas WORTHY and Sarah Gannaway. Sur. John Gannaway.

13 December 1800. Samuel WRIGHT and Barbee Glover Mason, dau. of William Mason, deceased. Sur. John Mason. Married 18 December.

19 December 1786. Joseph YARBROUGH and Temperance Walton, dau. of George Walton. Sur. Fr. Watkins. Married 12 Jan.

15 April 1805. Joseph YARBROUGH and Polly Ellington, dau. of John Ellington who consents. Sur. Forrest Farley. Married 7 May.

21 July 1782. Thomas YORKSHIRE and Polly Nokes. Ministers returns.

1 December 1789. Drury YOUNG and Winnie Palmer, dau. of Reuben Palmer. Sur. William Baldwin.

29 August 1797. James YOUNG and Oney Burks, dau. of John Burks who consents. Sur. William Burks. James son of Stephen Young.

21 July 1806. John YOUNG and Jennie Crenshaw. Parent John Gounter (Grinter?) is surety. (Whose parent).

30 June 1798. Johnston YOUNG and Sarah Thomason, dau. of Arnold Thomason who is surety. Married 3 July.

1 December 1797. Thomas Elaba YOUNG and Martha Hurt, dau. of Benjamin Hurt, deceased and Martha Hurt. Sur. Josiah Hurt. Married 7 December.

8 March 1785. Charles ZACHARY and Tishee Baldwin, dau. of Caleb Baldwin. Sur. Thomas Baldwin. Married 2 July.

INDEX TO BRIDES

A

Adams,
- Palethia — 16
- Martha — 16
- Mary — 52

Akin,
- Barshala — 79
- Frances — 85
- Nancy — 5
- Patsy — 70

Allen,
- Elizabeth — 1; (2) 71
- Hannah — 38
- Martha — 14, 72
- Martha V. — 66
- Mary — 7
- Nancy — 14
- Sally — 27

Anderson,
- Elizabeth — 46
- Mary — 23; 65
- Mildred — (2) 47
- Patsy — 29
- Sarah Weldon — 2

Andrews,
- Ave — 23
- Frances S. — 75

Anyan,
- Sally P — 10

Archdeacon,
- Alice — 53
- Mary — 58

Armes,
- Frances — 79
- Lucy — 29

Armstrong,
- Jane — 83

Arnold,
- Nancy — 37
- Rhoda — 35
- Sally — 86

Aston,
- Ann — 50

Atkins,
- Elizabeth — 13
- Sarah — 20; 21

Atwood,
- Elizabeth — 77
- Martha — 18

Atwood,
- Ann — 69

Ayers;
- Frances — 39

B

Bailey,
- Prudence — 14
- Sally — 61

Baker,
- Eliza — 5
- Elizabeth — 6
- Elizabeth G — 76
- Jean — 82
- Jenny — 20
- Judith — 20
- Kitty G. — 37
- Lucy — 39
- Martha — 83
- Mary — 70
- Molly — 20
- Nancy — 30, 56
- Patsy — 33
- Sally — 43, 76
- Susanna — 33

Baldwin,
    Abigail 16
    Agnes 35
    Ann 21
    Elizabeth 35
    Martha 15
    Mary Ann 75
    Nancy 4
    Patsy 65
    Susannah 34
    Tishee 88

Barksdale,
    Elizabeth 72

Barnett,
    Betty 30

Barton
    Eleanor 76
    Elizabeth 76
    Mary 84

Bassett,
    Martha (2) 43

Baugh,
    Caroline 53
    Priscilla 74

Baulding,
    Martha 15
    Sarah 64

Beadle,
    Priscilla 62

Bean,
    Elizabeth 69

Beasley,
    Nancy 3
    Winnie 40

Bell,
    Elizabeth 20
    Sally (2) 25
    Violet 20

Bennet,
    Agnes (2) 22
    Clara 44
    Lucy 31
    Polly 15

Berry,
    Ann 62
    Elizabeth 52
    Jenny 24
    Lucy 7
    Mary 71
    Sarah 18

Berryman,
    Frances 12

Bibb,
    Nancy 9

Bidditt,
    Massey 1

Biggars,
    Martha 39

Bigger,
    Betsy Coleman 40
    Elizabeth H C 70
    Lucy S 7
    Polly 14, 74
    Susanna 14, 67

Binns,
    Nancy 35

Bird,
    Betsy 15
    Diana 24

Black,
    Ann 63
    Elizabeth 73
    Isabell 76
    Janey 66
    Martha (2) 66

Blanton,
    Elizabeth 20
    Patsy 37
    Peggy 20

Boaz,
- Molly — 50
- Nancy — 23

Booker,
- Elizabeth Julia — 32
- Frances — 64
- Jane Davis — 56
- Lucy — 8
- Mary — 9, 15
- Nancy — 55
- Rebecca — 73

Boulding,
- Abigail — 16

Bowman,
- Jane — 44
- Lucy — 27

Bracher,
- Martha — 85

Bradshaw,
- Polly — 12
- Sally — 59

Branch,
- Prudence — 85

Brightwell,
- Amy — 52
- Betsy — 33
- Nancy (2) — 11
- Rachel — 68
- Rhoda — 49

Broadway,
- Mary D — 21

Brooks,
- Agnes — 84
- Martha — 27
- Mary — 45
- Nancy — 58
- Nelly — 61
- Sarah — 12
- Susanna — 58

Brown,
- Betsy — 51
- Kizzey — 4
- Polly — 82
- Sally — 62

Bruce,
- Lucy — 68

Bryan,
- Susanna — 43

Bryant,
- Dicey — 15

Buchanan,
- Jane — 61

Burk,
- Mildred — 65

Burke,
- Betsy — 8
- Mary — 54

Burks,
- Edith — 46
- Elizabeth — 73
- Millincer — 52
- Oney — 88
- Susanne — 60, 72

Burnett,
- Sarah — 51

Burton,
- Elizabeth — 85
- Judith — 73
- Magdalene — 82

Butler,
- Fanny — 64
- Hannah — 5

Buxton,
- Penelope — 75, 76

Bynum,
- Mary — 30

C

Caldwell,
- Elizabeth — 83
- Jane — 71
- Janey — 74
- Mary — 13
- Polly — 8
- Sally — 57
- Violet — 3

Calhoon,
- Ann — 31
- Peggy — 1
- Rebecca — 7
- Violet — 50

Cannon,
- Elizabeth — 41
- Luvenia — 57

Cardwell,
- Lucy — 15
- Mary — 14

Carson,
- Susanna — 63

Carr,
- Mary — 15
- Rebecca — 85

Carrier,
- Sarah — 57

Carter,
- Ann — 8
- Elizabeth — 27, (2)77
- Jensey — 77
- Lucy — 36
- Mary — 5
- Mildred — 2
- Millie Wade — 80
- Nancy — 9, 10
- Nancy Waddell — 76
- Polly — 2, 18
- Sally — 11, 22, 49

Cason,
- Amelia — 3
- Betsy — 30
- Judith — 17
- Lucy — 7
- Mary — 3

Cawley,
- Rebecca — 66

Cawthon,
- Nancy — 62

Cawthorn,
- Elizabeth — 33
- Margaret — 26
- Nancy — 62
- Peggy — 17
- Polly — 28, 82
- Sally — 30, 82

Chaffin,
- Ann — 82
- Cusey — 59
- Cuzy — 59

Chambers,
- Cussias — 1
- Elizabeth Ann — 75
- Mary Susanna — 58

Chapman,
- Tabby — 6

Chappel,
- Martha — 30
- Sally — 70

Chapple,
- Dolly — 3

Cheadle,
- Mary Woodson — 40
- Polly — 40

Childers,
- Elizabeth — 41
- Nancy C — 57

Childress,
    Frances   83
    Naomi   13
    Obedience   23

Christian,
    Sarah Winston   81

Chumbley,
    Frances   46, 48
    Martha   69

Chumley,
    Anna   53
    Sarah   1

Claiborne,
    Betsy   82

Clark,
    Ann   47
    Lucy M   81
    Mildred   5
    Susanne   49

Clarke,
    Agnes   69
    Betsy   45
    Elizabeth   34, 50, 63
    Polly   29
    Sally   7, 29
    Susanna   68

Clibourn,
    Martha   17
    Sally   22

Cobb,
    Frances   44, 49

Cody,
    Martha   16

Coffee,
    Elizabeth W   42

Cole,
    Isabel   72

Coleman,
    Betsy   40

Collier,
    Mary   17

Collins,
    Sarah   32

Cook,
    Ann W   42
    Conny (2)   54
    Polly   75
    Sally   55

Crenshaw,
    Jennie   88

Crockett,
    Molly   28

Cunningham,
    Elizabeth   70
    Jean   50
    Judith   14
    Letty   53
    Mary   34
    Nancy   48
    Susannah   9

D

Dabney,
    Anna H   35
    Sarah Glenn   42

Daniel,
    Betty Ann   66
    Jane   14, 19
    Mary   24

Davenport,
    Nancy   41

Davidson,
    Avey   76
    Elizabeth   11
    Mary   42
    Phebe   10
    Sally   5, 11
    Sarah   8

Davis,
    Anne   37
    Elizabeth   6, 53
    Fanny   71, 72
    Jane   67
    Lucy   49
    Mary   67

Davis, cont
    Nancy Berry   19
    Polly J   31
    Sally   5
    Sarah   30, 32

Davison,
    Nancy   11
    Patsy   35
    Polly   35

Dawson,
    Martha   18

Day,
    Sally   5

Dejarnette,
    Dicey   81
    Elizabeth   27
    Marrimiar   37, 38
    Nancy   34
    Susanna (2)   65

Deshazer,
    Nancy   39
    Martha (2)   42
    Susanna   36

Dick,
    Sally (2)   77

Dickenson,
    Jenny   39

Dillon,
    Fanny   65

Dixon,
    Betsy   63

Dodd,
    Elizabeth   6

Donald,
    Mary   24

Dowdy,
    Mary Ann   51

Downs,
    Margaret P   34

Drinkard,
    Obedience   22

Duncan,
    Sarah   46

Dunnivant,
    Anna   59
    Elizabeth (2)   73
    Frances (2)   13
    Mary   80
    Nancy   25

Dupuy,
    Janey Watkins   23
    Nancy   31
    Sally   18
    Susanne   81

E

Edwards,
    Martha (2)   84

Eillbank (?),
    Elizabeth   44

Elam,
    Jane   53
    Lucy   40
    Patsy   58
    Polly   67

Elebank,
    Sarah   75

Ellett,
    Tabitha   55

Ellington,
    Elizabeth   9
    Frances   25
    Mary Chappell   87
    Nancy   54
    Patience   22
    Polly   88
    Prudence   4
    Rebecca   54
    Sibbeller   7

Elliott,
    Nancy (2)   65

Ellitt,
    Sarah   18

Ellyson,
    Sally   35

Estes,
    Betty Ward   60
    Frances   3
    Rachel   15

Evans,
    Alee   5
    Martha   62

Ewing,
    Eleanor   20
    Elizabeth   20, 21

F

Farmer,
    Elizabeth   84
    Martha   70, 72
    Riette   26
    Ruth   26

Fears,
    Elizabeth   23
    Sally   38
    Sarah   39

Ferguson,
    Fannie   64
    Mary   78
    Nancy   86

Fielder,
    Martha   64
    Patsy   33

Finley,
    Elizabeth   31

Fleming,
    Elizabeth   47
    Lucy   60
    Martha   23

Flournoy,
    Ann Farish   85
    Julia   27
    Lucy F   57
    Marcia M   57
    Mary   65

Fore,
    Betty   67
    Elizabeth (2)   6
    Judith (2)   69
    Mary   17

Forrest,
    Elizabeth   21
    Mary W   2
    Nancy   48

Foster,
    Elizabeth R   9
    Elizabeth   75, 80
    Judith T   2
    Mary (2)   51
    Nancy   22, 68
    Sarah H   11
    Susanna (2)   54

Fowlkes,
    Elizabeth   36
    Louisa   59
    Mickey   18
    Polly   23
    Rossy   23

Franklin,
    Betsy   83
    Elizabeth   37
    Martha   51
    Polly   64
    Sally   40

Frazer,
    Mary   10

Fuqua,
    Elizabeth   73
    Patsy   75

G

Gallahorn,
    Nancy   25

Gannaway,
    Sarah   87
    Tabitha   49

Gaulding,
    Elizabeth   60
    Jemima   53
    Judith   41, 60
    Lucy   58
    Martha   30
    Polly   18, 69
    Sally   84
    Susanna   86

Gears,
    Jency   74

Geers,
    Nancy   38
    Polly   36
    Sally   34

Gibbons,
    Polly   71
    Sarah   49

Gibson,
    Agnes   44
    Martha H   61
    Mary   28

Gilchrist,
    Susannah   63

Giles,
    Nancy   74

Gillespie,
    Anne   74
    Frances   69
    Lucy   9

Gilliam,
    Martha   35, 54
    Polly   82
    Sally   37
    Susanna   87

Glenn,
    Betty Ann   56
    Dorothy   78
    Elizabeth   78
    Martha   86

Going,
    Nancy   41

Goode,
    Frances   25
    Lucy   33
    Mary   12
    Susanna R   60

Goslin,
    Sally   65

Gowing,
    Nancy   41

Graham,
    Jane   71
    Margaret   72
    Mary   72
    Sarah   7

Gray,
    Caty   34, 35
    Lucy   18
    Sally   30

Green,
    Betsy   6
    Elizabeth   80
    Lucy Davis   80
    Rosana   59

Greer,
    Betsy   10

Griffin,
    Mary (2)   5
    Sally   73

Grissell,
    Elizabeth   76

Guill,
    Elizabeth   47
    Jenny   71
    Lucy   75
    Mary   11
    Rhoda   3

H

Hamblen,
- Elizabeth — 10
- Elizabeth Ann — 28
- Sarah — 17

Hambleton,
- Elizabeth — 79
- Esther — 79
- Mary — 64

Hamilton,
- Ann — 14
- Elizabeth — 76
- Jane — 44
- Rebecca — 33

Hamlett,
- Hannah — 17
- Martha — 46
- Mary — 43
- Sally — 77

Hamlin,
- Jennett S — 12

Hankins,
- Elizabeth — 28

Harper,
- Lucy — 62
- Martha — 60
- Mary — 59
- Milly — 58

Harris,
- Ann Skip Magdalen — 62
- Judith — 64
- Prudence — 3

Harrison,
- Jane — 24

Hart,
- Mary — 57

Haskins,
- Ann N — 81
- Elizabeth — 22, 48, 79
- Jane — 47, 70
- Lucy — 55
- Martha — 27
- Mary — 47
- Nancy — 78

Hatton,
- Elizabeth — 44

Hawkins,
- Mary — 7
- Polly — 50
- Sarah — 79

Hays,
- Mary Ann — 15

Henderson,
- Elizabeth — 22

Hill,
- Anne — 21
- Betty — 78
- Doshea — 76
- Elizabeth — 33
- Jane — 55
- Judith — 2
- Margaret — 19
- Mary — 4
- Phoebe — 16
- Polly — 42, 81
- Sally — 11
- Susannah — 82
- Thirsa — 52

Hines,
- Elizabeth — 2
- Martha — 47
- Nancy — 38
- Winnie — 10
- Sarah — 29

Hix,
- Frances — 9, 10

Holcombe,
- Mary — 2
- Sarah — 47

Holland,
- Nancy — 56
- Sally — 64

Holloway,
   Agnes   32
   Judith   30
   Priscilla (2)   86

Holt,
   Dicey   87
   Sally   28
   Sarah   78

Hood,
   Sally   25

Hopkins,
   Susan T   70

Hossley,
   Lucy   2

Hoskins,
   Ann   63

Howard,
   Frances   51

Howell,
   Betsy   1, 3
   Catherine   25
   Lucy   52
   Mary   48

Hubbard,
   Betty   33
   Judith   7
   Nancy (2)   4

Hudgins,
   Sally   36

Hudson,
   Elizabeth   1
   Elizabeth D   27
   Frances   37
   Jensey   60
   Pamala   1
   Penelope   60
   Polly   44, 68
   Polly B   55
   Prudence   16
   Sarah   25

Hughes,
   Peggy   33

Hundley,
   Anne   86

Hurt,
   Elizabeth   86
   Judith   15, 71
   Martha   88
   Mary   71
   Oney   68
   Rachel   6
   Sally   27
   Sarah   74

Huskerson,
   Lucrecy   14
   Luc   15

J

Jackson,
   Magdalen   44, 45
   Mary Ann   78
   Milly   29
   Nancy   42
   Obedience   68
   Patsy   41
   Peggy R   18
   Sally   82
   Sarah   39
   Tabitha   28

Jeffries,
   Nancy   56

Jennings,
   Lucy   26
   Nancy   57
   Polly   61
   Sally   22

Johns,
   Elizabeth   46
   Sarah   61, 69

Johnson,
- Agnes — 74
- Elizabeth — 26
- Elizabeth Kerr — 1
- Nancy — 31
- Polly — 19
- Tabitha — 83

Jones,
- Fanny — 24
- Lucy — 32
- Sarah — 31
- Susanna — 68

Jordan,
- Elinder — 47

K

Keeling,
- Polly — 12

Kelley,
- Susanna — 32

Kelly,
- Christiana — 17
- Lucy (2) — 60

King,
- Delia — 69

Kitchen,
- Sally — 32

Kuling,
- Polly — 12

L

Lancaster,
- Ann — 87
- Elizabeth — 51
- Frances — 45
- Judy — 45
- Molly — 33
- Polly — 61
- Sally — 31

Lanewell,
- Tabitha — 60

Lawrence,
- Frances — 83

League,
- Fanny — 55

Le Grand,
- Drucilla — 45
- Judith — 46
- Lucy — 18
- Mary Sneed — 8
- Sarah — 70

Leigh,
- Catherine — 67
- Ellen — 87
- Sarah — 48

Leneave,
- Susanna — 14, 15, 45

Le Nene,
- Susanna (2) — 46

Lewelling,
- Lucy — 59

Lewis,
- Elizabeth — 53, 67
- Mary — 7
- Nancy — 26

Lightfoot,
- Elizabeth (2) — 50

Ligon,
- Lucy — 60
- Nancy — 29
- Phebe — 71
- Sarah H — 54

Little,
- Darkus — 53

Lockett,
- Lucy Jane — 8
- Patsy — 57
- Polly — 56

London,
    Sally   72

Lowdon,
    Sally   70

Lowe,
    Elizabeth   69

Lumpkin,
    Nancy   19

Mc

McCargo,
    Letty   56
    Susanna   57

McDearmon,
    Creasey   21
    Elizabeth   35
    Mary   21
    Sarah   85

McGehee,
    Elizabeth   2, 38
    Fanny   48
    Judith   81
    Mary   30, 82
    Nancy   9

McRobert,
    Elizabeth   14

McTaggart,
    Frances   77
    Nelly   40
    Peggy   40

M

Mackdearmon,
    Elizabeth   36

Malloy,
    Sarah   17

Mann,
    Margaret   54

Manning,
    Susannah P   1

Marrable,
    Elizabeth B   42

Marsh,
    Jerusha   72

Marshall,
    Nancy (2)   79
    Patience   79
    Polly T   43
    Rodith   47

Martin,
    Ann   27
    Betsy   59
    Elizabeth (2)   51
    Mary V   2
    Mildred   85
    Polly   31
    Sarah   14

Mason,
    Barbee Glover   88
    Mary   52
    Nancy   68
    Peggy   25
    Sarah   78
    Elizabeth   39

Massey,
    Rebecca   85

Mathews,
    Agnes   54
    Ann   44, 49
    Betsy   37
    Frances E   18
    Lucy   37
    Patsey   31
    Susan P   85

Mattox,
    Elizabeth   12

Maxey,
    Biddeth   3

May,
    Jane   28

Meadows,
    Judith   17
    Martha   (2)   43
    Nancy   87
    Patsy   22
    Polly   58
    Rosanna   58
    Sarah   19
    Sythe   17

Meredith,
    Dolly   82

Michaux,
    Betsy   17

Miller,
    Anne D   80
    Elizabeth   81
    Mary H   33, 40
    Patsey   24
    Sally   57

Mills,
    Anne   75
    Hannah (2)   49

Mitchell,
    Agnes   28
    Ann   61
    Christian   40
    Fanny   41
    Rebecca   49

Montagert,
    Sarah   32

Moon,,
    Betsy A   11
    Polly V   55

Moore,
    Anne   51
    Betsy A   11
    Elizabeth   84
    Polly V   55
    Sally   50
    Sarah (2)   51, 52

Morain,
    Catherine   10

Morgan,
    Nancy   72
    Rebecca   24
    Sarah   74
    Susanna   25

Morris,
    Ann   64
    Nancy   77
    Polly   53
    Susanna   24

Morrison,
    Hannah   74

Morrow,
    Esther   84
    Jane   53
    Peggy   84

Morton,
    Agnes   51, 73
    Ann Smith   67
    Elizabeth   10, 87
    Lucy   49
    Mary   29
    Nancy   76
    Sally   30
    Sarah   62
    Susanna   77

Mosby,
    Ann   55
    Patsy   3

Moss,
    Tabitha   46

Muraine,
    Martha   72

Murray,
    Alley   27
    Edith   45

Murrain,
    Esther   50

Muse,
    Olive   50

N

Nash,
- Ann — 36, 43
- Elizabeth F — 66
- Elizabeth Fisher — 72
- Martha Wallace — 8
- Susannah F — 46

Neal,
- Polly (2) — 4

Nelson,
- Betsy — 78
- Mary Hill — 13
- Milly — 20

Nimmo,
- Elizabeth — 34

Nokes,
- Polly — 88

North,
- Dolly — 43
- Frances — 37
- Mary — 16, 67
- Nancy — 51
- Polly — 44, 45
- Susanna — 5

Nunnally,
- Martha — 84

O

Odineal,
- Edy — 65

Oliver,
- Ann B — 17
- Elizabeth — 41
- Lydia — 42
- Mary — 74

Osborne,
- Nancy — 79
- Priscilla — 6

Overstreet,
- Ann M — 52

Owen,
- Aggathy — 13
- Anne — 68
- Elizabeth — 76
- Jane Archer — 6
- Jane — 8
- Jemima — 68
- Kesiah — 61
- Milly — 67
- Phoebe — 10
- Polly — 13
- Polly T — 68

P

Palmer,
- Elizabeth — 82
- Winnie — 88

Palmore,
- Frances — 46

Pamplet,
- Elizabeth — 41

Pankey,
- Judith — 58
- Nancy — 42
- Susan W. — 58

Paris,
- Patty — 22
- Polly — 22

Parkinson,
- Mary — 69
- Nancy — 36

Parks,
- Margaret — 82
- Mary — 19

Parrott,
- Susannah — 39

Pate,
    Judith   79

Patterson,
    Maryan   34

Paylor,
    Susanna   75

Peck,
    Polly   54

Peek,
    Agnes   54, 61
    Hetty   71

Pendleton,
    Lucy   64
    Sally   60

Penick,
    Ann   13, 64
    Betsy   4
    Elizabeth Comer   62
    Fanny   73
    Hope Ann   70
    Jane (2)   41
    Jerusha   8
    Judith   29, 39, 50
    Keziah   3
    Lucy   8, 83
    Martha   65
    Nancy   9, 77
    Patsey   65
    Phebe   18
    Polly Walker   4
    Sally B   69
    Tabitha   56

Pennill,
    Patsy   62

Perkinson,
    Betsy (2)   13
    Clarissa H   54
    Eliza   9, 10
    Elizabeth   47, 87
    Harriet H   80
    Patsy   48, 53
    Sally   56

Perryman,
    Milly   12

Pettus,
    Elizabeth   18
    Martha   57
    Mary   63

Philips,
    Elizabeth   29
    Lucy   58
    Mary H   73
    Nancy   61
    Sally   52

Porter,
    Anne   14
    Eleanor   84
    Jane Ewing   77
    Peggy   87
    Sarah   55

Price,
    Betsy   78
    Elizabeth   87
    Fanny   64
    Mary   21
    Nancy   44, 52
    Patsy   4
    Polly   4, 28
    Susanna   67
    Tabitha   18

Pucket,
    Nancy   49
    Sukey   49

Pulliam,
    Betsy   29
    Nancy   87

Purnall,
    Mary   23

R

Raine,
    Polly   56

Rains,
    Nancy   68

Redd,
- Ann — 81
- Elizabeth — 8, 16, 70
- Martha — 44, 58
- Mary Ann — 40
- Nancy — 51
- Polly — 49
- Sally — 16
- Sally A — 36
- Susannah — 53

Reed,
- Elizabeth — 76

Rice,
- Ann — 13
- Drucilla — 78
- Frances — 15, 35
- Jane — 8
- Lucy — 48
- Lydia — 25
- Martha — 65, 66
- Mary (2) — 26, 83, 84
- Massey — 59
- Molly — 23
- Nancy — 21
- Patsey — 57
- Rachel — 74
- Sally — 59, 76

Richards,
- Betsy — 7
- Daphne Taylor — 57
- Patty — 39
- Polly — 39

Richardson,
- Mary — 67

Richerson,
- Betty Ann (2) — 73

Richie,
- Agnes — 19
- Christian — 34

Ritchie,
- Agnes — 31
- Christian — 55
- Margaret — 76

Roberts,
- Betsy — 69
- Elizabeth — 11
- Sally — 84

Robertson,
- Frances — 27
- Magdalene — 36
- Mary Magdalene — 35
- Rebecca — 86
- Sarah — 84
- Mary — 12

Robins,
- Elizabeth — 7

Robinson,
- Elizabeth — 3
- Mildred — 26

Rogers,
- Caroline — 28

Routledge,
- Mary — 20

Rowlett,
- Elizabeth — 30
- Frances — 35
- Jemima — 39
- Julia B — 23
- Mary 10
- Nancy — 68
- Prudence — 61
- Sally — 31
- Sarah — 22

Rudd,
- Oney — 74
- Sally — 16
- Tabitha — 61

Rudder,
- Nancy Meadows — 86

Russell,
- Mary — 10
- Patsy — 48

Rutledge,
- Elizabeth   13
- Judith (2)   39
- Mary   20
- Nancy   21
- Prudence   39

S

Sadler,
- Fanny   16
- Nancy   59

Scott,
- Agnes   48
- Elizabeth Archer   46
- Martha   19
- Martha Williams   57
- Mary   56
- Susanna Elizabeth   16

Selby,
- Mary   33

Self,
- Judith   86

Shackleton,
- Mary   29

Sharp,
- Susanna   28

Shelton,
- Henrietta   71

Shepard,
- Fanny   85

Sheperd,
- Franklin   85

Shepherd,
- Elizabeth   26
- Mildred   33
- Patsey   32

Sheppard,
- Mary   79

Shepperson,
- Betsy   66
- Mary   20
- Nancy   25

Sherron,
- Jennett   12

Shewmaker,
- Masdal   80

Shields,
- Elizabeth   66

Short,
- Elizabeth   26

Simmons,
- Anne   34
- Annie   5
- Easter   71
- Frances   86
- Judiah   43

Smith,
- Elizabeth   3,37,47,83
- Elizabeth A   84
- Ellenor   62,67
- Hannah   46
- Henrietta   38
- Mary   10
- Mary Ann   37,80
- Nancy   12,45
- Polly   43,80
- Sally   29,53
- Sophia   36
- Susan   79
- Susannah   12
- Tabitha   73

Smithson,
- Martha   45

Spaulding,
- Judith   38

Spencer,
- Elizabeth   21
- Frances A   85
- Frankie   38
- Mary Ann   2
- Sally   80

Standefer,
    Leah   30

Steel,
    Jean   19

Stewart,
    Peggy   1

Stowers,
    Frances   52

Summons,
    Frances   75

Sweeny,
    Frances   80
    Polly   21

Swinney,
    Tillilicum   45

T

Talley,
    Elizabeth   67

Tanner,
    Elizabeth   16

Tate,
    Katherine   75

Taylor,
    Betsy   86
    Judith   2
    Elizabeth   78
    Sarah   23

Thackston,
    Polly   73

Thaxton,
    Elizabeth   83
    Peggy   25

Thomason,
    Sarah   88

Thompson,
    Elizabeth   34, 37
    Jane   4
    Mary   39
    Nancy   42
    Polly   46
    Susannah   63

Thornton,
    Dorothy   44
    Harriet Susanna   11
    Jane C   78

Tredway,
    Sarah   16

Trowers,
    Mary Ann (2)   32

Truman,
    Mary   66

Tucker,
    Lena   55
    Patsy   9

Tuggle,
    Nancy T   69
    Polly   66
    Sally   18

Turner,
    Edith   48

Tyree,
    Anna   36
    Elizabeth   9
    Judy   32

V

Vaughan,
    Elizabeth   72
    Mary   12
    Sally   62

Venable,
- Agnes — 32, 38
- Anne — 31, 65
- Betsy Ann — 81
- Clementina — 66
- Dolly — 32
- Elizabeth — 84, 86
- Elizabeth W — 81
- Martha — 38, 79
- Martha W — 21
- Mary — 52
- Mary C — 86
- Nancy — 19, 48
- Patty — 12
- Peggy R — 13

W

Waddell,
- Frances — 24
- Polly — 6
- Ritte — 24
- Sally — 26

Waddill,
- Molly — 2
- Sally C — 24

Waddle,
- Lucy — 48
- Mary Ann — 63

Wade,
- Betsy — 6
- Frances — 30
- Lucy — 50
- Mabala — 66
- Patty — 32
- Polly — 63

Walker,
- Betsy W — 26
- Elizabeth — 23, 55
- Frances — 46
- Judith — 26
- Lucy — 87
- Lucy C — 19
- Mary W — 1
- Patsy — 71

Wallace,
- Elizabeth — 60
- Mary — 54

Walthall,
- Elizabeth — 36
- Martha — 6
- Nancy — 36

Walton,
- Dishea — 80
- Eliza S — 23
- Molly — 22
- Nancy Hughes — 55
- Patty — 45
- Sally — 7, 81
- Sukey — 57
- Susanna — 57
- Temperance — 88

Ward,
- Anne — 27
- Martha B C (2) — 83
- Mary — 38

Watkins,
- Elizabeth — 56, 78
- Frances — 81
- Martha H — 48
- Mary — 40, 41
- Maryann — 60
- Milly — 62, 63
- Patsy — 58
- Polly — 17
- Rhoda — 13, 15, 65
- Susan M — 20
- Temperance — 40

Watson,
- Ann — 67
- Elizabeth — 45
- Hannah — 14, 82
- Mary — 82, 87
- Nancy — 1
- Polly — 5
- Susanna — 19, 72

Weakley,
- Susannah — 49

Weaver,
- Ann — 50
- Ann Crafford — 27

Webber,
- Mary — 24
- Sally — 41

Webseter,
- Lydia — 68

Wells,
- Prudence — 53

White,
- Sarah — 50

Whitwoorth,
- Elizabeth — 41
- Mary — 17

Whood,
- Elizabeth — 43

Wiatt,
- Sally — 8

Wilkerson,
- Betsy — 14
- Nancy — 75

Wilks,
- Elizabeth — 28

Williams,
- Lucy — 80
- Micha — 21
- Nancy — 52

Williamson,
- Elizabeth — 8
- Lucy — 63
- Nancy — 59
- Phoebe — 25
- Polly — 73
- Rebecca — 35

Wilson,
- Sally — 82

Wimbish,
- Nancy — 56
- Sarah — 30

Waldridge,
- Mary — 38

Womack,
- Betsy — 20
- Cressy — 74
- Elizabeth — 19
- Nancy — 24
- Patty — 63
- Patsy — 85
- Polly — 5

Wood,
- Ann — 12
- Betsy — 63
- Mary (2) — 37
- Sarah — 11

Woodall,
- Elizabeth — 56
- Frances — 75

Woodcock,
- Sarah Dean — 63

Woodridge,
- Mary — 38
- Nancy — 6

Woodrum,
- Jane — 52

Woodson,
- Agnes — 81
- Elizabeth — 47, 78
- Judith — 31
- Mary — 27, 38
- Nancy — 38
- Patsy N — 43

Woolridge,
- Mary (2) — 41
- Rhoda — 70

Wooten,
- Betty — 29
- Jemima — 81
- Keziah — 22
- Lucy C — 71
- Nancy — 64
- Nancy O — 34
- Patty — 47
- Polly R — 29

Wooton,
- Lucy — 14
- Mary G — 34

Worsham,
- Elizabeth — 85
- Elizabeth B — 10

Y

Yarbrough,
- Nancy Hughes — 45

Young,
- Betsy — 38
- Charlotte — 43
- Elizabeth (2) — 40
- Mary — 11
- Mildred — 42
- Nancy — 66
- Polly — 55, 64
- Rebecca — 26
- Sarah — 42
- Tabitha — 36

Z

Zachary,
- Judith — 76